Structuring for Success in the English Classroom

Structuring for Success in the English Classroom

Classroom Practices in Teaching English
1981–1982

Candy Carter, Chair,
and the Committee on Classroom Practices

National Council of Teachers of English
1111 Kenyon Road, Urbana, Illinois 61801

Grateful acknowledgement is made for permission to reprint the following material: "Metaphors " (p. 116) from *The Collected Poems* by Sylvia Plath, edited by Ted Hughes. Copyright © 1960 by Ted Hughes. Reprinted by permission of Harper and Row, Publishers, Inc. "This Is Just to Say," from *The Collected Earlier Poems of William Carlos Williams*. Copyright 1938 by New Directions Publishing Corporation. Reprinted by permission of New Directions Publishing Corporation. "The Dance," from *The Collected Later Poems of William Carlos Williams*. Copyright 1944 by William Carlos Williams. Reprinted by permission of New Directions Publishing Corporation.

Staff Editors: Jane Curran and Barbara Davis

Book Design: Tom Kovacs, interior; V. Martin, cover

NCTE Stock Number 47607

Library of Congress Cataloging in Publication Data
  Main entry under title:

Structuring for success in the English classroom.

  Bibliography: p.
  1. English language—Study and teaching—Ad-
dresses, essays, lectures.   2. Language arts—
Addresses, essays, lectures.   I. Carter, Candy,
1947–   .   II. National Council of Teachers of
English. Committee on Classroom Practices.
PE1065.S83   428'.007'1073   82-2309
ISBN 0-8141-4760-7   AACR2

Contents

3 Structuring the Writing Assignment

4 Structuring the Evaluation of Writing

Preface

Last year's Committee on Classroom Practices publication focused on the problem of "Dealing with Differences" in the English language arts classroom. Participants in our open meeting in Cincinnati on November 21, 1980, agreed that "differences" was only part of a more general problem. English teachers today are faced with increased demands on their time and energy, while expectations for student success have also risen. Old terms that we thought were buried with Univac computers and Ipana toothpaste in the fifties came up: discipline, classroom management, organization, and structure. This time, however, the emphasis seems to have shifted. Rather than structure for regimentation, the word *structure* now implies success—success for both the student and the teacher. Clear guidelines, explicit expectations, the committee felt, would help both teacher and student work toward common goals.

After the meeting, the call for manuscripts was issued in *Language Arts, English Journal, Council-Grams, College English,* and *English Education,* as well as in the journals of many NCTE-affiliated organizations.

By April 15, 100 manuscripts had been submitted from throughout the United States. The manuscripts, with authors' names removed, were evaluated by committee members Jean Procope-Martin, James Lalley, Patricia Phelan, and Yetive Bradley—a committee representing several geographic areas and grade level viewpoints.

Thirty-one manuscripts representing these varying viewpoints were finally selected and submitted to the NCTE Editorial Board for approval to publish. All represent methods of structuring a total classroom or class assignment in such a way that success, if not guaranteed, is the most likely outcome.

Structuring for Success in the English Classroom

Introduction

"Mrs. C, I can't decide. *You* tell me what to do." When I first heard that statement from a student, I was appalled at his ingratitude. I had given him a choice in an assignment, a hand in his own destiny, and he wanted me to tell him what to do! I had spent four somewhat miserable years in high school yearning for just such an opportunity, and this ingrate was passing up the chance of a lifetime.

Or so I thought. The more time I spent in the classroom, however, the more I came to realize that freedom, those wide open options made available to students in the educational revolution of the late sixties and seventies, often led to confusion and failure rather than excitement and stimulation. But was a return to the mindless drills, the pat literary interpretations, the formula essays that we had rebelled against in the sixties the answer, either?

At about this time, I was fortunate to take a course from Sharon Belshaw, a woman who became a mentor to many of us in northern California. Sharon showed that structure need not inhibit creativity and often would encourage it. Structure makes a difference: it helps clarify your expectations of students, it assists students in making decisions without telling them what to do, and it increases students' chances for success.

The class with Sharon led to a significant change in my teaching. The choices are still there, but they are pared down, clarified. My standards for students are no longer a hidden agenda. It should come as no surprise that my students' work has improved as a result of these changes. Their efforts are not only technically better, they are more imaginative. The security provided by the structure of the assignment gives students the freedom to take their creativity to the limits, simply because they know what the limits are.

Across the country, structure has returned to the classroom in the wake of the "back-to-basics" movement. Sometimes, the return to structure is a tragedy: once again, students are beginning on page 1 of the grammar book on September 5 and ending on page 527 on June 11. More often, however, teachers have learned some lessons over the last twenty years of pendulum swinging. We have learned that a lack of

3

structure does not improve student or teacher performance and in many cases inhibits it. We have learned that "schools without failure" does not also have to mean "schools without goals." We have learned that structure does not have to equal boredom and the death of creativity. The articles presented under the six divisions of this book—Structuring the Classroom, Integrating the Curriculum, Structuring the Writing Assignment, Structuring the Evaluation of Writing, Structuring Language Study, and Structuring Reading and the Teaching of Literature—illustrate the success of initiating this structure in the classroom.

The educators who have contributed to this volume have shown how we have emerged from the "back-to-basics" backlash with a new type of structure in mind for our classrooms, a structure for success.

Candy Carter
Sierra Mountain Intermediate
    School
Truckee, California

1 Structuring the Classroom

Structuring Small Groups for the Secondary English Class

Steve Athanases
Arlington High School, Arlington Heights, Illinois

The small group process is not a new technique. Its rewards are well known: the drawing out of reticent students, increased sharing of ideas, improved listening. In their text *Student-Centered Language Arts and Reading, K-13,* James Moffett and Betty Jane Wagner cite stimulation and support among peers as other benefits. In addition to these general rewards, small groups in the secondary English class can fulfill needs related to specific course content:

1. connecting literary themes to students' personal lives and world
2. creating character analyses of literary figures
3. generating composition topics
4. brainstorming arguments to prepare for persuasive writing
5. critiquing peer compositions

However, without a clear process for implementation, small groups too often fall short of these goals and can simply be a waste of time. Students frequently see group work as an "easy hour" because there is seemingly little pressure to perform for the class and teacher. To insure that students are thinking and working individually and as group members, objectives and tasks must be carefully structured in advance and members must be made clearly aware of their responsibilities for each step of the process.

Insuring the Success of Small Groups

Groups must be small. More than four or five members make groups feel like crowds—which causes too many individuals to withdraw. Teachers may assemble groups to create fairly equal distribution of students with various talents and abilities. When possible, groups should be coed. If close friends are a problem, they should be separated. Students assembling their own groups should also consider these factors.

7

Moffett and Wagner point out that common sense is the basis for effective small group work and that rules for participant involvement should be kept to a minimum, particularly after students have had group experience. In *The Dynamics of Discussion: Grouptalk,* Babette Whipple outlines some simplified rules for groups in general to insure discussion, listening, relevancy of comments, response, and summarizing on the part of group members. To achieve some of these goals in small groups of high school English students, the following steps have been designed. These steps can easily be mastered and repeated by students.

1. To insure that all members have something to contribute, students are to consider the problem or assignment and perform note taking before meeting in groups.

2. Once in groups, members must determine who will fill the following roles:
   a. Discussion leader (to keep the discussion moving)
   b. Recorder (to make notes of key comments from members)
   c. Speaker (to present group results to class)
   Group members may volunteer for these positions or may be selected by peers for their potential to fulfill the roles.

3. Preliminary group discussion is systematic to insure that everyone contributes: leader asks each member to share any notes and additional thoughts; recorder takes notes.

4. Group members may now respond, discuss, argue, vote, select, and so forth.

5. Recorder reads final notes to group; members add comments so notes accurately represent group work.

6. Each group speaker presents the group thoughts to the class in a cohesive, convincing, emphatic manner. (If in list form, group work is recorded on the board.)

7. One class member records all group comments.

8. From this record, a ditto is created with overall class thoughts in list or summary form.

9. Copies from ditto are distributed the next day to students for their perusal, further comment, and possible use in later work.

Examples of Small Groups

Small groups may be used in a variety of ways in the secondary English classroom. The following examples illustrate three possible situations in which small groups are an effective teaching tool.

Character Analysis

Students read John Steinbeck's *Of Mice and Men.* The character George is assigned to half the class, Lennie to the other half. Students begin listing traits of their character, citing passages from the text for support. Three "George" groups and three "Lennie" groups are formed; group members share their work, building on one another's comments— agreeing, disagreeing, and always illustrating with examples.

Goal. Which group(s), as represented by the speaker's presentation to the class, can create the most insightful and thoroughly documented portrait of its assigned character?

Result. Students are exposed to character analysis and use of supporting evidence. They become better prepared to write such analyses in later exposure to literature.

Argumentation

Three or four pairs of groups are formed. Within each pair, one group argues the pro and one the con of some school-related debatable issue:

> The school paper has printed a scathing review of this year's school musical. The director and various cast members are irate; the editorial staff defends its freedom to print opinion. The issue becomes: What is the role of a school newspaper? Group A: Support the stand of the editorial staff; Group B: Argue against that stand.

Goals. Which side of each issue can most thoroughly and convincingly present its argument to the class? In which arguments can loopholes be found?

Result. Students see more clearly how to build and organize argument and how to check for flaws. They become better prepared to organize and to write their own persuasive compositions.

Generating Composition Topics

Students view "The Sixties," a brief film montage of that decade (available in many school districts or through educational film distributors). In discussion, the class categorizes the array of images presented in the film: political figures, fads, famous criminals, music, social conflicts, sports heroes, major historical events. The class discusses trends of the sixties that emerge from these categories of images. Students break into groups to brainstorm lists of images from the seventies that fit the same categories.

Goal. Which group can present lists of images that most colorfully and incisively paint a portrait of the seventies?

Follow-Up Assignment. "A Thesis for the Seventies." From all of the class lists, select a group of images that are in some way unified or show a trend of the seventies. Write a thesis sentence that states that trend. Use the examples to develop a convincing composition.

Result. Students enjoy a lively look at cultural dimensions of their time. The students are enthusiastic about these compositions because they've been created organically—generated by work in the groups.

Small group work, if carefully structured, not only aids students as communicators, but can effectively illustrate and inspire the class, making seemingly abstract or dull concepts and practices more accessible, and therefore valuable, to students.

References

Moffett, James, and Wagner, Betty Jane. *Student-Centered Language Arts and Reading, K-13,* 2nd ed. Boston: Houghton Mifflin, 1976.

Whipple, Babette. *Dynamics of Discussion: Grouptalk.* Belmont, Mass.: Porthole Press, 1975.

The Broccoli and the Cheese Sauce:
An Experiment in Team Teaching

Cynthia A. Miller
Austin College, Sherman, Texas

At the National Developmental Studies Conference in November 1980, Dr. John Roueche delivered a keynote address in which he suggested a variety of ways for educators to reach out to basic skills students and offer them support and encouragement. In the realm of instruction, Dr. Roueche stated that just as such foods as broccoli can be made more appetizing with cheese sauce, so can courses perceived as "difficult" or "tedious" be made more palatable with the introduction of creative instructional approaches. When we (the coordinator of the basic skills writing program and the coordinator of the basic skills speech communication program) designed a team-taught writing class using speech communication activities and prewriting conferences to facilitate writing assignments, our main goal was to enable students to acquire the basic skills necessary to succeed in the freshman level GSD 101 writing course. If putting cheese sauce on the broccoli helped, then we were willing to give it a try.

In this article, we would like to share ideas that make our team-taught class a success. First, we want to offer a general overview of the basic skills program at Southern Illinois University at Carbondale (SIUC) and, specifically, our team-taught class. Second, we want to discuss how speech activities were used as a springboard for writing assignments and explain our conference procedure. Third, we want to share the values of interrelating writing and speech communication in a team-taught class.

Description of the Course

Students enrolling at SIUC who have an ACT score of less than eighteen or who have grade averages that place them in the bottom half of their high school graduating class must enter the university through the Center for Basic Skills (CBS). After taking a battery of tests, students are placed in CBS writing, mathematics, speech communication, and/or reading and study skills. The eighteen students placed in our team-taught writing course were required to take the one-hour CBS course before enrolling in freshman English. Students were informed that the course would be taught by a writing instructor and speech communication instructor and that exercises would accompany writing projects. However, the focus of the course would be on composition assignments, and speech-related activities would not be graded.

During the semester, both instructors attended the class. Originally, the speech instructor was to be primarily responsible for classroom exercises, and the writing instructor was to be primarily responsible for lectures on the writing process and for grading papers. Fortunately, this format never materialized. The writing instructor frequently initiated innovative activities, and the speech communication instructor found she could lecture on outlining an audience analysis, and so forth. During each other's ten- to fifteen-minute lectures, both instructors offered ideas and clarifying information. The grading responsibility also became a shared process. Initially, the speech communication instructor read all the papers and put a penciled grade on them; the writing instructor reread the papers and decided on the final grade. We then discussed our criteria for our grading and, in most cases, found we agreed. We eventually divided the papers in half and cut down on the grading load.

During the first half of the semester (eight weeks), we met with the entire class. The students wrote only paragraphs. Various speech activities were used to help students generate ideas, organize their thoughts, and revise their first drafts. Before the students engaged in the exercises and took "risks" in front of the class, they became acquainted with each other. A relaxed, informal class atmosphere contributed to the students' participation.

During the second half of the semester (seven weeks), the students wrote essays, and instruction became more personalized. The remainder of the semester was divided into three conference periods. The class was divided in half, and the students were assigned to one of the instructors. During each conference period, students met with their instructor at least twice and discussed their essay topic. The students wrote several drafts outside class, discussing each draft with their instructor until they were satisfied with the writing and ready for a grade. At the end of each conference period, we met as a class, completed essays were handed in, new assignments were made, and appointments were scheduled for the next round of meetings. Each student began a new essay assignment at the beginning of each conference period while revising the previous essay. At the end of the course, three essays were required.

Speech Activities and Writing Assignments

Having presented a general description of the course, we would like to share speech communication activities we used to kick off writing assignments and our conference system. Before the explanation of each exercise, the objectives for the assignment are outlined. The primary objectives are related to composition; however, secondary objectives emerged and are significant because they involve the improvement of communication skills.

Exercise: Interviewing

Objectives

1. To generate material for a paragraph
2. To narrow a topic
3. To become better acquainted with each other
4. To ask open-ended questions and to respond fully to questions

Activity

The entire class brainstormed and developed a list of questions they wanted to ask one another. These questions were written on the board. The students paired off and asked each other some or all the questions on the board, jotting down their partner's responses. From the responses to the questions, students were asked to select one facet of the other person's life (hobbies, family, travels). Each student was asked to write out a list of questions that pertained specifically to one area of the other person's life. During the second interview session, the students took turns asking their new sets of questions and jotted down the information. Now the students were ready to write a paragraph on a particular aspect of the other person's life.

Exercise: Storytelling

Objectives

1. To recognize the audience in written and oral communication
2. To understand the prewriting process
3. To outline main ideas
4. To use time-order sequence
5. To use transition words for changes in time and place
6. To develop confidence in speaking before a group

Activity

The students were asked to write about their most embarrassing moment (any personal experience will do). The entire class brainstormed for ideas, and students were free to choose an idea on the board or from their own personal experience. Using outline form, the students arranged their stories in chronological order. In their progression of ideas, they used transition words to move from one idea to another. Each student gave a three- to five-minute speech from his or her outline. The class gave positive feedback and, in some instances, suggested changes such as more transitions, clarifying information, or rearrangement of events. Using the feedback from the audience, the students reworked their outlines and wrote paragraphs using chronological sequence with transition words and phrases.

Exercise: Role Playing and Letter Writing

Objectives

1. To adapt oral and written messages to an audience
2. To understand the revision process
3. To identify and analyze the audience before making formal written or oral messages

Activity

Two students volunteered for a role-playing situation. They were asked to pretend that they were two friends exchanging information about their weekend. Because the two students knew each other, they abbreviated events, used slang, and jumped from one idea to another. Next, one student sat down and the other student told the instructors the same story. This time, the student used more formal grammar and sentence construction, employed a wider vocabulary, and explained events in detail. As a class, we discussed how the audience influenced the style and diction of oral communication.

Following this exercise, we handed out copies of three letters. Each letter centered around the same situation—a student had committed a traffic violation and was ticketed. However, each letter explained the incident to a different person—a friend, parent, or school administrator. As a class, we discussed how the audience affected the written communication. There were obvious differences in diction and style as the letters became more formal.

Next, we brainstormed ways in which students might get into trouble in school. The class selected one situation and composed three letters explaining the incident to a friend, a parent, and a school official. Before the letters were graded, the students paired off and proofread one another's papers for mistakes. During this time, the instructors were available for aid in revising (we marked sentences containing mistakes and told the students to identify and correct the errors). The students rewrote the letters and submitted their final drafts.

Exercise: Show, Don't Tell: Nonverbal Communication

Objectives

1. To understand the differences between showing and telling
2. To generate supporting material for a main idea
3. To increase awareness of nonverbal communication

Activity

In a ten-minute lecture, we elaborated on various types of nonverbal communication such as facial expression, eye contact, gestures, and body language. We also discussed how nonverbal communication demonstrates feelings. For example, anger may be expressed by knitted eyebrows, squinted eyes, or doubled fists.

Each person was given a slip of paper listing a different emotion and was asked to act out or express the emotion without speaking. The students used body language, facial expression, and eye contact to communicate the feeling while the audience identified the emotion.

After this preparation, students were ready to write a "Show, Don't Tell" paragraph. The assignment was to describe a person's nonverbal communication. Each person observed someone else in a particular situation and then wrote a topic sentence identifying that person and what he or she was feeling (for example, "My English teacher was depressed"). The remainder of the paragraph was to describe in detail the person's nonverbal communication, which showed how the person felt. The students read their paragraphs aloud to the class without the topic sentence, and the other students tried to identify the feeling.

Prewriting Conferences

During the second part of the semester, students met at least twice with an instructor during each of the three conference periods. The first prewriting conference for each assignment was called "Talking It Out." The following format was used to record the student's ideas:

Name _____

Conference One: Talking It Out

General Topic:

Possible Thesis Statements:

1.

2.

3.

Final Thesis Statement:

The general topic for each essay was recorded at the top of the page. If the students disliked the suggested topics, they were free to come up with another topic. At the beginning of the session, we asked the students to talk about any thoughts and feelings related to the topic. We asked open-ended questions (what, why, how), paraphrased, and used "door-openers" ("Go ahead, tell me more about it") to get students to discuss their ideas. Students also were asked to identify different ways of focusing on the subject. They were able to formulate two or three possible thesis statements for the paper, and each selected the thesis statement offering the greatest possibilities. (For example, Fred, a heavy smoker, wanted to write about smoking. After he explored the general topic aloud, he realized there were several possible directions for his essay. He articulated three possible thesis statements: "This paper will give me new insights into smoking"; "There are many effects smoking has on the human body"; "There are many ways to quit smoking." Fred selected the latter statement as the focus of his paper.) At the end of the conference, students were asked to think about and jot down ideas on their particular themes.

At the second conference, "Organizing and Elaborating on Ideas," students talked about their thoughts and feelings on their specific topics. The same strategies listed before were used to draw out ideas. Next, the students selected the main points they wanted to bring out in their essays. When the students could articulate their main ideas, these ideas were listed on the following conference form:

Name _____

Conference Two: Organizing and Elaborating on Ideas

Thesis Statement:

Main Ideas:

1.

2.

3.

4.

Supporting Material for Main Ideas

1. Main Idea:

   Support:

2. Main Idea:

   Support:

3. Main Idea:

   Support:

4. Main Idea:

   Support:

We asked students to give examples, reasons, facts, and so forth to support their main ideas. The supporting statements were recorded, and a rough outline of the body of the essay emerged. The students were ready to write their first drafts, adding an introduction and conclusion. The students usually scheduled conferences to talk about revisions of their first draft. Even after the next assignment was given, students were encouraged to rewrite their first essay until they were ready to receive a grade.

Value of a Team-Taught Writing Course

When writing and speech communication teachers interweave their subject areas, students build and reinforce communication skills. Students learn that writing and speaking involve an audience and that the emphasis in any communicative situation is on relating effectively to others. By talking out and organizing their ideas before they begin to write and later by rewriting drafts, students learn communication as a process. Their focus is no longer on the final product but on the experience of producing that product. Students also learn that organization is essential to both formal written and oral messages. Both forms of communication call for an introduction, body, and conclusion, and there must be main ideas and supporting statements within the body of the essay or speech. Whether classes are team taught or taught by a single instructor, students need to have basic oral and written communication skills reinforced.

Personally, the experience of team teaching was invaluable. We were able to give students special attention and personalized instruction. We learned about each other's subject area: the writing instructor feels confident in creating and implementing exercises in class, and the speech communication instructor feels secure helping students with their writing. Finally, the paper crunch that usually accompanies writing classes did not develop. Because we continually talked to students about their papers, we were already familiar with their final drafts. By dividing up the papers, we still could give careful attention to the papers while cutting back on paper work.

Teachers of basic skills students need to demonstrate the interrelatedness of all basic skills—reading, writing, and speaking. A team-taught class is one way to accomplish this task. This approach brings depth to courses and enhances instruction.

Structuring for Success in the Freshman English Classroom: A Strategy for International Students

Laura S. Armesto
Barry University, Miami

Perhaps the single most important factor requiring changes in the structure of the freshman English classroom today is the influx of international students. As colleges seek to ease the financial crunch by accepting more and more of these students, freshman English instructors face an increasingly complex task: how to meet the composition needs of students who score below 300 on the verbal portion of the SAT or below 600 on TOEFL?

Experience with these students in the classroom indicates that their deficiencies are primarily in analytical skills and only secondarily in grammatical and syntactical skills. For the most part, international students are products of educational systems where conceptual analysis and discussion are the exception and lectures and memorization are the rule. Given such training, these students are at a disadvantage in an English classroom where they are expected to read and analyze literature and to write analytical essays of their own.

It is all very well to teach rhetorical patterns as a means to organize writing, but it is useless if students have no thoughts to organize. Instead, international students must first be taught to analyze so that they can have something to write about.

At Barry University, international students are placed in a special section of freshman composition where the major objective is to sharpen analytical skills. A standard composition textbook, Laurie G. Kirszner and Stephen R. Mandell's *Patterns for College Writing: A Rhetorical Reader and Guide,* a thesaurus, and an English-English dictionary are used.

Before each class session, students must read the introductory material explaining the rhetorical pattern at hand and one essay. They are instructed to read thoroughly, to make notes of particularly difficult or interesting points, and to look up unfamiliar words. In other words, they are to be prepared to ask questions. Creating the habit of active participation in the learning process is crucial for international students whose

19

classroom experience has been one of passive listening. For this reason, class should be conducted through questions and answers rather than lectures.

To illustrate, we can use the first unit in the Kirszner and Mandell text, narration. The students have been assigned to read the introduction, which explains the objectives of narration, the structuring of the essay, and some of the finer points in writing narratives, such as the use of verb tenses and transitions. In addition, they have read the first essay in the unit, John M. Bresnahan's "Monday, March 5, 1770: Who Was to Blame?" which narrates the events of the Boston Massacre.

I begin class by asking the students questions about the introduction. When do we use narration? What is this pattern designed to communicate? I continue the questions, explaining and amplifying where necessary, until I am sure that students have a firm grasp of narration as a rhetorical pattern. Then, I move on to Bresnahan's essay.

I cover the first three or four essays very systematically, in a series of four steps:

1. I begin by asking, "What is said in paragraph 1? 2? 3?" and so forth, until all paragraphs have been discussed. The students answer aloud, sometimes arguing a point and many times asking the meaning of particularly difficult words or idioms. As the discussion progresses, I list the events on the blackboard: Paragraph 4: crowd; Paragraph 5: (nothing); Paragraph 6: fire bell. . . .

2. Once students have abstracted the major events in the narrative, I return to the beginning of the essay by asking, "Since the narration of events begins in paragraph 4, what is the function of paragraphs 1, 2, and 3?" Once we determine that these paragraphs are introductory, I ask where in those paragraphs is there a general statement of the topic that the essay covers? Discussion then elicits the thesis—its purpose and its placement.

3. With the thesis clarified, students are now ready to return to the events listed on the blackboard and to outline the body of the essay. At this point, it is important that students be taught to look for patterns. This, again, is done through questions. Asking "Why does this happen?" and "What brought this event about?" eventually leads students to see that this particular essay deals with causes and effects. After they have outlined it as such, with causes and effects as primary supports and the events as the secondary supports, they are ready to look again at the conclusion and discuss the author's effectiveness in supporting the thesis. "Is the essay clear? If so, why? If not, why not?" By noting how well the author has or has not organized the supporting evidence, linked the events by means of

transitional devices, and used detail, students gain a sense of the mechanics of effective writing. In addition, they have analyzed the content and learned how a conclusion is reached logically.

4. The last step in the process is for students to write an abstract. Because the essays in the Kirszner and Mandell book are generally short, abstracts are rarely longer than one paragraph. I explain to the students that the abstract is an essay in miniature, that they will simply reduce the essay to its essential points. I use the following abstract structure superimposed on traditional paragraph structure:

1. Sentence 1: Topic sentence must include four points:
   a. title
   b. author
   c. method used by author
   d. author's thesis

   For example, in *"Monday, March 5, 1770: Who Was to Blame?"* (a), *John M. Bresnahan, Jr.* (b), *narrates* (c) the events leading up to the Boston Massacre in order to determine *whether the British were guilty of murder or acting in self-defense* (d).

2. Sentences 2 – ?: Developmental (body) sentences, one for each of the primary supports (in this case, cause and effect) and as many as needed to paraphrase the secondary supports.

3. Last sentence: Concluding sentence, giving student's evaluation of how effectively the author has communicated the information.

I have found it useful to do the first abstract on the blackboard with students contributing the wording. This method works particularly well to introduce the finer points of paraphrasing. At first, as we look at the sentences in the essay, I point out key words that must be paraphrased. Students look them up in their dictionaries and thesauri, and we choose from several alternatives. Then we move on to altering the sentence structure and finally decide on a sentence of our own. Although time consuming, this collective effort is valuable because it teaches how to paraphrase, reviews grammatical structure, and helps students learn to use the dictionary and thesaurus. Most of these students will at first exhibit a tendency to overuse the thesaurus, thinking that paraphrasing is a matter of finding synonyms for each and every word in the original. However, once they learn that paraphrasing requires altering sentence structure too, this problem diminishes.

I follow this process exclusively for the first three weeks of the semester, with students writing abstracts individually in class, where I am available to provide individual assistance. The class consists of a two-hour block three days a week with rarely more than twenty students enrolled. At first, I give students the entire second hour to write, but gradually I decrease the amount of time available for writing.

After the third week or so, students write a variety of papers, all using the abstract as a starting point and the essays in the text to provide topics for analysis. From the abstract, we move to answering essay questions in a simulated studying-and-taking-the-exam situation. George Orwell's "Shooting an Elephant" is a particularly good essay for this exercise. After they discuss, outline, and prepare an abstract, students must answer the question, "In what way(s) was shooting the elephant an enlightening experience for the narrator?" Although Orwell narrates the events in his experience, it is only by analyzing that students can give an answer.

From the essay question, we move on to the essay proper, but not as writing exercises using rhetorical patterns in a vacuum. Instead, we write position papers, reflections, reactions, observations, and evaluations, all using analysis, abstraction, and paraphrasing coupled with correct structuring and patterning (be it comparison-contrast, process, or cause and effect), until we cover all the patterns.

This approach has been successful for several reasons. First, it teaches rhetoric not as an end but as a means. Students are not asked to write one essay using each pattern in a vacuum. Instead, they learn that patterns are options to be chosen depending on the topic and how they wish to organize it for most effective communication. Second, this approach teaches students to analyze, to look beyond the obvious, and to form their own conclusions. Many students have told me that learning to read in this fashion has proved a great help in other courses; they read faster and understand more, and by being able to abstract the really important points, they study better for tests. Third, it teaches them to paraphrase, giving them some sense of connotation and denotation, the nuances of language, and the variety of sentence structures available to them. Paraphrasing also results in a dramatic increase in vocabulary as well as excellent preparation for writing the research paper.

These skills, of course, are cumulative, and not all students progress at the same speed. To test progress, I use a series of short articles from news magazines or newspapers. Every two weeks or so, students outline and abstract one of these articles, using only their dictionaries and thesauri, and write the type of paper we have been practicing during the previous two weeks. In this way, I can identify problem areas and give students additional practice where needed before going on to the next unit. All papers are marked for content, structure, and grammar, and students correct them with me in class. Grades are based on progress with a minimum of seventy as passing.

This approach is a simple and common-sense one. Its success depends on careful structuring and systematic exposition. It is time consuming for the instructor because students write during every class period and frequently have outside assignments as well. But because students are getting constant practice and individual attention, they are learning skills that not only fulfill the freshman English requirement but help them write and study in other courses as well. Perhaps the greatest benefit is that with the availability of a course such as this, international students need not be relegated to remedial labs or, worse yet, to the rear of the classroom in frustration.

Reference

Kirszner, Laurie G., and Mandell, Stephen R. *Patterns for College Writing: A Rhetorical Reader and Guide.* New York: St. Martin's Press, 1980.

The Question of the Day

Rose Sallberg Kam
Encino High School, Sacramento, California

One aid to classroom order is to begin every class period with a five-minute task for students to complete while the teacher takes roll and completes other necessary beginning-of-period activities. Journal writing, quick quizzes, vocabulary review, and sentence modeling are four such period starters. Another that I have found useful is the Question of the Day.

The purposes of the Question of the Day are to review and reinforce rules of capitalization, spelling, punctuation, and grammar; to encourage completion of a week-long rather than a one-period activity; and to start each class period positively and productively. Side benefits, however, include students' developing a wider awareness of the world, doing better proofreading on other assignments, and being delighted in spotting the use of unusual capitalization and punctuation by other writers.

The easiest way to introduce the activity is to have the date, a Question of the Day, and a rule of grammar already on the chalkboard and to give students a dittoed or photocopied form for use all week. The form contains these directions at the top:

> Daily, during roll, copy the date, question number, Question of the Day, and rule of grammar, spelling, or punctuation from the chalkboard. For credit, the *question* must be copied *exactly*. It is a model of the rule. Your answer may be a phrase or a sentence, as long as your meaning is clear. You may shorten the rule as long as it is clear to you.

The rest of the form is divided into three columns: one column for the date and the question number, a second (the largest) column for the question and its answer, and a third column for the rule of grammar, spelling, capitalization, or punctuation being exemplified. Horizontal lines divide the paper into a box for each day of the week.

During the first week of this activity, it is good to ask a quick series of proofreading and rule-comprehension questions as soon as the roll has been taken. For example, if I had put on the board: *April 20, 1981. # 1. Why is President Reagan's health mentioned in the news so often these days? RULE: Capitalize titles used as part of a name,* I might ask the following proofreading questions: Do you have "Why" capitalized? "President"? "Reagan's"? Have you spelled "Reagan's" R-E-A-G-A-N-'-S? Did you end with a question mark? (Even after two or three weeks of losing points for failure to copy *exactly,* some students still omit end punctuation or start with a lower case letter.) Then, to be sure that the day's rule is understood, I ask where the rule appears in the question. I also check for recall of other rules. For example, why are the words *Why* and *Reagan's* also capitalized? Why does the apostrophe come before the *s* in "Reagan's"?

Questions may be drawn from current events (international, national, state, local, school, the classroom itself) or may be general information questions to which students can readily obtain the answers. For example, "Who is the German god for whom Wednesday is named?" Since the purpose of the activity is to reinforce rules and not to stump students, I make it easy for them to locate the answers, adding such hints as, "Try a dictionary" or "Look at the bulletin board" (for a news clipping). I would accept as correct answers to the Reagan question "He was shot three weeks ago," "He had lung surgery," "He just left the hospital," and so forth. "Woden" would suffice as an answer to the Wednesday question.

My scoring system is two points per day (ten possible per week). Although the date and rule are required on the week's sheet, the two points cover only the question and answer. *Any* error in the question causes loss of that point. If any answer contains a mechanical error but is correct and can be understood clearly, I circle the error but give the student the point. Teachers using larger numbers of points might award points for including the dates and rules.

In response to the Question of the Day, the vast majority of students quickly become competitive (or at least curious) and settle down to copy the question and answer it promptly. Roll taking is performed so quickly that within a short time, the activity rarely takes more than five minutes, even including oral review of the rule and calling for additional examples of its use.

Papers are due each Friday. At first it takes me ten minutes to correct a set of thirty-five papers; after a week or two, I can see at a glance that date and rules have been done, and read only the questions and answers. Another option on paper correcting is to take time on Mondays to have students correct each other's papers from the previous week before beginning the new set. This requires that the teacher carefully read aloud each capital letter, punctuation mark, and so forth, but it can be very useful in clearing up any misunderstandings and in reinforcing rules.

Identical format on all papers speeds correcting time, so I do not recommend having students use their own paper.

Even if the Question of the Day did not arouse the interesting discussions in the classroom that it has, I would still find it a simple activity for reinforcing mechanics. I know it's working in other ways when a student asks why Isaac Asimov capitalized "Them" and "Us" in *Fantastic Voyage,* or when a student whispers, "I've got a good question for you!"

Varying Whole Class Instruction

Sharon S. Norby
North Branford High School, Connecticut

Working with above average high school sophomores in a year-long, American literature course is both demanding and rewarding. These students require constant challenges to hold their interest and to promote independent perceptions, logical deductions, and meaningful learning experiences. One such competitive class inspired the following instructional exercise, which eventually became a mainstay of my various teaching techniques.

Comparing and contrasting writers, time periods, and reading matter is an approach that can become either futile or fruitful. To offset the superficial lists that might result from such an exercise, an open forum was established where half the class became "experts" on one writer in a given period and the other half on a second writer. Each group utilized biographical material, an example of the writer's work, and the critical reaction by the writer's peers to gather in-depth information about its assigned writer. In a classroom discussion, the opposite group quizzed the first group to learn as much as possible about the writer. Then the opposite group was questioned about its writer. Writers paired in this manner included James Fenimore Cooper and Washington Irving, James Russell Lowell and Henry Wadsworth Longfellow, and John Smith and William Bradford.

As the exercise was repeated, the questioners became more astute—probing, seeking logical deductions and inferences from their fellow classmates. The "experts" began to take their knowledge of the individual seriously—interpreting, questioning, looking beyond the text for additional explanatory information.

I initially presented students with an outline of the information for which they should be responsible. Later, however, the outline was enlarged by the students as each strove to add something new or relevant or a "tidbit" of his or her own finding. Constructive competition among students was keen—bringing much more to the study of these authors than a teacher-directed, note-taking, reading-quiz approach ever could.

I now eagerly look forward to using this teaching technique each year, and it has rarely failed the class. Students will need time to develop the necessary skills as well as the confidence and the enthusiasm that the lesson requires. However, from its first use in the fall until the final round in the spring, this practice gives the teacher valuable information on the growing awareness and overall intellectual development of individual students through their participation and involvement.

After the presentations, students usually write an essay on the comparisons and contrasts they found most evident, intriguing, or enlightening. In this way I may see what information has been internalized. Not surprisingly, organization and information seem to flow more smoothly, even for those students whose writing skills are not as proficient as others. Overall, the success of this approach has been nothing short of excellent.

One Holistic Approach to Teaching Writing

Michael W. Raymond
Stetson University, DeLand, Florida

The marketplace poses paradoxical but all too familiar stresses upon advanced writing curricula. On the one hand, diminishing resources for education cause college departments to be understaffed and to reduce the number and frequency of writing course offerings. On the other hand, the job market (and the students' accompanying anxiety) demands both greater emphasis on communication skills and more courses in writing for the technical, legal, business, and teaching vocations. One frequent outcome of such stress is departmental "discussion" (or is it warfare?) of what is to be offered (and subsequently who is and is not to stay). In many cases the issue becomes a question of which one or two kinds of advanced writing a department will offer: technical, business, expository, or creative.

Usually these discussions serve only to increase paranoia, to alienate colleagues, and to dissipate teacher energies. Regardless of the outcome of the discussions, each persuasion scurries about defending its particular territory, hawking or shuffling data on full-time equivalences, employment opportunities, and other cost-benefit ratios. No demand of the marketplace is served; no one emerges with more than a partial victory.

One way to avoid dissipating the energies meant for teaching advanced writing is to avoid altogether the discussions over pedigree. There is little need for separate courses in creative, technical, business, and expository writing. Rather than making fine distinctions about nomenclature, emphases, tones, and audiences, we could be teaching writing. Rather than offering separate specialty courses that students can take only once, we could be teaching a spiral of courses—each of which integrates creative, technical, business, and expository writing. A holistic approach to advanced writing could satisfy the humanistic needs of the faculty as well as the paradoxical demands of the marketplace.

The following is a description of one advanced writing course that has adopted successfully the holistic approach. At Stetson University—a small private university particularly sensitive to such demands—the English

29

Department has heard not only the administrators' cries of financial anguish and the students' begging for "real world" skills but also its faculty arguing over pedagogy. As a result, we began moving to holistic writing courses. The standard advanced expository writing course now integrates technical, business, expository, and creative writing within a single unified approach.

The course uses as texts Richard Lanham's *Style: An Antitextbook,* a rhetorical reader, and a technical and business writing manual. Lanham provides the theoretical explanation for a holistic design of a writing course. He asserts that writing should be taught as style "for and as what it is—a pleasure, a grace, a joy, a delight" and that writing seeks "*to define a situation* and a personal role within that situation."[1] The rhetorical reader provides thematic units on broad issues with which to structure the course. Typical units include diverse readings on such issues as happiness, heroes, male-female roles and relationships, work, and the future. The technical and business writing manual provides instruction on and examples of specific writing techniques.

The process of a typical unit begins with the students considering the readings on the issue of that unit. Their attention is not only on analyzing form and content of another's writing but also on developing a thesis that they may use for their own writing in that unit. The thesis may be a direct response to the reading, a spin-off occasioned by the unit's readings, or any idea connected to the unit's issue, but it should be developed thoughtfully because it remains the thesis for all of the writing for that unit. As the unit progresses with classroom instruction and discussion, students submit separate technical, business, expository, and creative assignments that present their particular thesis on that unit's issue.

Usually the creative assignment comes first because students are allowed total freedom in their selection of strategy or genre. This encourages experimentation or a concentration in an area of particular interest as well as energy for working up the unit's thesis. The technical, business, and expository assignments are specifically prescriptive in style and format.

The consciousness of distinctions in pedigree diminish as students respond to the challenges of writing—to adapt to and to experiment in a variety of verbal contexts. For example, the unit on heroes includes readings on Janis Joplin, Jerry Brown, and a successful immigrant and requires a creative paper, a technical manual, an inquiry letter, and a semantic argument essay. A senior pre-law student developed a rather cynical thesis that public officials are politicians who carefully construct a public artifice that disguises their private personalities. Her creative piece was the tandem of a political newspaper advertisement and a news story on political scandal; her manual was entitled "How to Operate a Winning

Campaign"; her inquiry letter asked for the politician's attendance at a senior citizens' banquet while emphasizing the group's high rate of voter registration; the essay used connotation ironically to praise President Carter's schizophrenic handling of inflation. For the same unit on heroes, a sophomore geology major argued that the sudden and transitory fame for a rock singer is destructive. Using puns and jargon from his major field, he wrote a rock song, a manual for servicing a rock star with women, alcohol, and drugs, an agent's letter asking a rock star to agree to a frenzied concert schedule, and a holier-than-thou attack by a parent on Alice Cooper.

The crucial part of such a course design (and its presentation in the classroom) is for the teacher to be convinced that an advanced writing course should aim primarily at an acute self-consciousness about style and to sell that aim to students who are accustomed to rigid nomenclature, absolute norms, and pragmatic exhortations.

Committed to the teaching of writing as a spiraling process that teaches writing over and over with increasing demands of sophistication, the English Department at Stetson University is encouraged with the success of this new approach. The students are taking pleasure in the course and seem more willing participants in the battle against "the chronic absence of mind in language use."[2]

The most apparent source of pleasure for the students is the course's built-in variety and renewed opportunities. Each unit has a variety of readings, a variety of instructional techniques, a variety of assignments, and a variety of ideas and attitudes. With the creative, technical, business, and expository assignments in each unit, the student has the opportunity to work successfully in a familiar area and to learn or improve in unfamiliar areas. As the term progresses and students gain experience in each area, they become more at ease in all areas. Furthermore, if a particular unit is not personally appealing, a student can look forward to the next unit with its new readings, new contexts, and new assignments. The variety within units and among units helps keep the course dynamic and challenging and reminds its participants that writing itself is dynamic and challenging.

The more subtle source of pleasure for the students is their growth in self-awareness. A constant in the holistic advanced writing course is the pleasure or satisfaction in recognizing and making choices, in developing an ability to adapt, and in sensing one's growing versatility. Rather than sensing that their one advanced writing course becomes a process of surrendering an entire term to the particular formulas of a specific pedigree, students sense that they are in control. They analyze ideas, styles, and structures. They choose their responses; they create their roles for the game playing; they become short-story writers, mechanical engineers, account executives, and class-action suit attorneys as the needs arise. Constantly juxtaposing forms and ideas from traditionally creative, technical, business, and expository writing, students become aware that they are writers—not just a creative writer or a technical writer or a business writer or an expository writer. They become verbally aware and comfortable with that awareness.

The awareness is not limited to versatility in writing. As Richard Lanham suggests, another awareness that develops with the "pleasure-and-context" approach to writing is the awareness of self as one who is a social dramatic role player and as one who is an individual. The holistic approach allows both senses of self to exist overtly and covertly in the course with the creative impulse of the initial paper and with the adaptation to the technical, business, and expository formats. Furthermore, the course can become an occasion to wrestle with individual and social identities. With the experimentation with styles comes experimentation with roles, with ways of thinking, and with ways of being.[3] With each unit the student gets to think about an individual personal position regarding some issue and to play three or four roles dictated by the assignments. Each unit can be an experiment in values and experiences in various career life-styles.

Thus, a holistic advanced writing course has assets for the multifaceted demands of the marketplace. It permits English departments to satisfy increasing demands for advanced writing courses that can train a diversity of students despite the constriction of resources. Perhaps, too, it can defuse those departmental discussions over which advanced writing course is to be offered. Its most important asset, however, is its service to the students. It provides a diversity of communications skills for students who are very conscious of the uncertain job market. Introduced to and proficient in technical, business, expository, and creative writing, the students are versatile and, perhaps more importantly, have a sense of their versatility.

Notes

1. Richard Lanham, *Style: An Antitextbook* (New Haven, Conn.: Yale University Press, 1973), pp. 20, 31.
2. Ibid., p. 7.
3. Ibid., p. 124.

Teaching ENG 101 along Natural Lines: The Structure of a Curriculum Based on Learning Theory

Rita Phipps
North Seattle Community College, Washington

Like most college English composition teachers, I want to turn out students who write not only competently but rigorously, with style, with ease, with expressiveness, with coherence, with clarity, and with an understanding of the connections or relationships among their ideas as they are expressed in sequential sentences and paragraphs. The problem is that it usually takes the whole quarter or semester to bring beginning composition students to the point at which they are starting to write well. The solution, then, is to speed up the composition process so that students begin to learn to write well early enough to practice and apply their new skills and become truly competent by the end of the term. Many teachers believe that students must write a lot to gain the level of competency we want for them, but even writing one paper a week for eight or ten or twelve weeks doesn't guarantee competence. One way to meet the problem is to have students write more papers than the finished ones they hand in. Papers that are not turned in are exchanged instead and are read and critiqued by other students, either in pairs or groups. While this generally is an effective way to have students produce a lot of writing, I have not been entirely satisfied with the overall progress they make towards achieving full competency.

Turning to learning and teaching theory for help, I discovered the cognitive theories of Benjamin Bloom[1] and Jean Piaget.[2] Now a dedicated convert, I am translating their theories into curriculum and teaching strategies, structuring the course in accordance with the sequence and causal chain their theories suggest. The most astounding result of my new curriculum, strategies, and structure is that the students' first finished papers are written with a firmer grasp of the inner workings of composition. Here are a few excerpts from their first narratives; the papers are by no means perfect, but they indicate a sophistication of structure:

> I prize my experiences with the forces of nature. One classic recollection remains vivid.

Paul and I arrived at the boat later than we had anticipated. The wind was already kicking up whitecaps that sprayed both boat and dock. . . . We spoke very little as we shoved off into the wind and spray.

Our plan had been to reach Sandpoint and then run with the Spinnaker to Kirkland for lunch. But once we were off I knew a more direct route was in store. . . .

As the C-lark approached shore I chose a private dock at random, handed the helm to Paul and crept forward apprehensively. . . .

We had soup and sandwiches for lunch while we jabbered about the exhilarating ride. Although once back at the dock confronted with the trip home against the wind, the matter [took on a different aspect]. . . .

Within five minutes of leaving the dock Paul was waving remnants of the rudder at me and screaming obscenities at the storm.

After fifteen minutes of floundering . . . a sloop offered assistance. I flung a line out for a tow and we clambered aboard. Not one moment of gratitude had passed before the C-lark lumbered over, turtled and began to sink under the pounding waves. . . . By this time the shore was in reach. . . . (Brad Jones)

"Ladies and gentlemen, please fasten your seatbelts. We are now landing at Meherabad International Airport." The pilot's voice echoed in the airplane. My heart was beating very fast. . . . I was going back home to Iran to visit after spending two years in the United States.

It was June of 1979 when I graduated from Roosevelt High School. I was very happy to leave school, but excited to start college. . . .

My summer was filled with going to school in the morning and working afterwards. . . . Towards the end of the [summer] quarter I got a phone call from my father in Iran. He wanted to arrange for me to come back and visit after summer quarter was over. . . .

The last day of the quarter I took my final exam. . . . Two days later I left for Iran. . . .

. . . When the plane landed I was the first one off. . . . (Siamak Dastmalchi)

The most major event in my life has just recently happened. I bought my first car. . . .

I'd been wanting to have my own car for quite some time. . . .

Finally, after a long search, a friend called and said he had a car for sale. . . . My friend told me about it; it'd been in an accident and needed new tires. . . .

On February 10, 1981, I picked up the car to do a little test driving. . . . On Friday, February 13, 1981, I paid cash for the vehicle. That same day . . .

Since that day, I've had to do only a few minor adjustments. . . . (Kris Coughlin)

Piaget has identified mental structures (mental capacities, conceptual frameworks) that are required for the performance of intellectual activities or operations.[3] For example, to perform the intellectual activity of analysis, a person must first develop such analysis-related mental structures as separating, ordering, classifying, comparing, contrasting, and so forth. Only after these requisite structures have developed can a person perform analysis. Piaget discovered that by the approximate age of thirteen all normally developed humans have developed all the mental structures needed to perform every intellectual operation or activity, including synthesis and evaluation. This is so, Piaget says, because the development of these mental structures is as inexorable and natural as the development of physical structures or physical maturation. Some people reach puberty earlier than others, but sooner or later all normally developed humans will reach puberty. Likewise, the development of mental structures follows the exigencies of natural cognitive or intellectual maturation and development processes.

Bloom, in a corollary way, has identified for teaching purposes six cognitive levels, from the lowest level of knowledge (mere remembering of facts) to the highest levels of understanding (synthesis and evaluation). When we put Piaget's linear, sequential structural maturation and development stages together with Bloom's hierarchical cognitive levels, we see that the mental structures of Piaget's first stage, the sensory-motor stage, are required for Bloom's lowest level (mere recognition of superficial functions and mere storage of data) and that Piaget's second-stage structures, those of the preoperational stage, are required for Bloom's second and third levels (low-level understanding that is required for applying one's superficial knowledge to analogous situations, for translating, for paraphrasing). Piaget's third age-related structures, those of the concrete operational stage (which make possible the activity of analysis), are required for Bloom's fourth level, the level of analysis. Piaget's final, fourth-stage structures, those of the formal operational stage (needed for synthesizing and evaluating), normally are reached when a human is approximately thirteen; those are the mental structures required for Bloom's last and highest levels: synthesis and evaluation (see Figure 1).

The implication of these theories is that, for example, an eleven-year-old (who has not yet naturally developed the structures needed for synthesizing) cannot synthesize or, in other words, cannot reach Bloom's fifth cognitive level. Yet this child does have the mental structures required for conducting analysis and thus is capable of reaching Bloom's fourth level. Consequently, fifth-grade teachers should be giving their eleven-year-olds the opportunity to exercise these structures by assigning them activities that require analytical operations and that accommodate individual differences in development.

The question for college teachers is, "If our adult students have the mental structures required for analyzing, synthesizing, and evaluating, why can't they learn to write in eleven weeks—or even in one week?" The

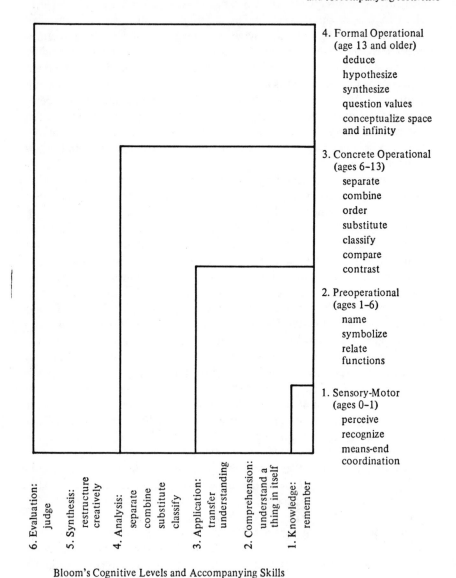

Figure 1. A model of the interrelationships between the cognitive theories of Benjamin Bloom and Jean Piaget.

answer is that while students do have the structures, they may never have applied them thoroughly enough to writing. If they haven't, our students must process the skill of writing through all of Piaget's structural stages, following the sequence in which the structures were first developed and used and omitting no step. This would be especially important if, as Piaget says, the structures are developed not only in a certain inevitable sequence but also in a causal chain, each one the cause or precursor of the next.

Intrigued by the implications of this hypothesis, I implemented it in my English 101 class. The results have been astounding. In one week, my students were able to write a narrative paper that demonstrated a firm grasp of the inner workings of that model, with transitions, complex but coherent structure, integrity of theme, and the *je ne sais quoi* that comes when writers know what they are doing and are enjoying doing it. Here is an example of one of the narratives written that second week (tense corrections are indicated by brackets):

> As I was sitting at home waiting for my fish to get done cooking, I wondered if it was worth all of the trouble I went through to get it.
>
> It was Sunday, the twenty-second, at three-thirty when I hooked that first steelhead. It was a mighty fighter, making my graphite rod bend like a fern in a storm. I patiently watched, while it shot out of the river, thrash the air, then plunge back into the icy water. Soon, the fish was tired from fighting, so I started reeling him in.
>
> While I was reeling him in, I thought back to all of the other steelhead that I had lost earlier in the day. First, I had lost two fish in the morning because my drag [had been] set too tight and they [had] snapped my twelve pound test line. Then, three more fish [had] spit their hooks. Finally, I had lost a sixth fish when my fishing buddy, Tim, [had] tried to kick the fish on shore, but [had] kicked it loose instead. After that, I [had been] broken-hearted.
>
> After about fifteen minutes [of reeling in my fish], I had the fish on shore. . . . I measured and weighed my prize, and it turned out to be a twelve-pound buck. . . .
>
> While I was cleaning my buck, Tim and I talked about all of the painstaking preparations we had made to make this fishing trip. We [had waked] up at three-thirty A.M., and [eaten] a breakfast of doughnuts and coffee. It is a sixty-five-mile drive to get to the Skykomish, but we had to go there because it was the hotspot of the season. . . . By eleven o'clock, rain had set in for the day. Even though it [had] poured, it hadn't discouraged the fishermen.
>
> After snagging the last of our driftgear, Tim and I set off for home. The miles seemed to pass in seconds, as I recalled my excitement of catching my first fish. After Tim dropped me off at home, I eagerly popped the fish in the oven. While it was cooking, I wondered if it was all worth it, but I knew it was after I took the first bite. (Jon Gregory)

While there are still grammatical and punctuation problems to work on, this student exemplifies the ease with which a rather firm grasp of structure can be learned in a relatively short time.

How did students learn to write skillful narratives in one week? On the first day, when students were at the first of Piaget's stages and at the lowest of Bloom's levels, I gave them this assignment: Write to the person sitting next to you. Start your paper by writing, "Dear _____, I want to tell you what I did for the thirty minutes before class." Here was their thesis statement and their audience (though I didn't label these as such yet). After they had written for about fifteen minutes, I put them into groups of four and gave them this assignment: These all should be narrative papers. Read the papers to each other and decide what a narrative paper is. After a lively discussion, they came up with the key elements of narration: events in time, in sequence. They had processed their new skill through the first stage or level: they knew what a narrative was and had basic knowledge of its key elements and function, albeit on a superficial level.

They were now ready to process their new skill through the next stage of mental structures (cognitive level) by applying their basic or superficial understanding and information to analogous situations. Their next assignment was to read an essay and to identify the sequence of events. The first story had a simple chronological sequence with the introduction and conclusion placed at a time later than the events occurring in the body—an envelope structure. Next they read a story in which the structure was a complex arrangement of flashbacks within flashbacks. In their small groups they were given the task of reconstructing the actual, literal sequence of events that had happened chronologically in real life. After this long and exciting application of their new knowledge, they could see clearly that an author can play around with time, restructuring and rearranging it at will. This application stage is critical because it provides students with a firm, concrete, internalized understanding of the new skill or subject, albeit still at a superficial level.

They were now ready to move to the concrete operational stage, the level of analysis. The next assignment: Think of your parents' life together. On each of these cards (I have handed out five to each student) write one event of your parents' life together. Then arrange and rearrange the pieces of paper listing events until you find an arrangement you think is logical and/or you feel good about. Then write a "curtain raiser" (introduction) and transitions to keep your readers informed about where they have been or where they are going and end the paper with a "curtain dropper" (conclusion).

Students performed these basically analytical operations. They then discussed their papers in small groups, identifying introduction, conclusion, transitions, and structure of events in each other's papers, and fully processed their new subject and skill through the analytical structures and the analytical level. As their understanding increased, the groups became very lively indeed, with everyone participating because all knew what was going on.

The next assignment called for processing the skill through the synthesizing structures; the students were now ready for Bloom's fifth level (synthesis). Their assignment, given on Thursday and due the following Monday, was an application of the skills gained in the previous exercises: Using what you have learned, write a narrative about an outstanding event in your life. On Monday the students returned to their small groups, and having worked at synthesizing activities since Thursday, they were able to evaluate each other's papers—and knew what they were doing. They gave advice, pointing out whether the knowledge from the first week had been used. Students then had the opportunity to rewrite their papers and hand them in on Wednesday. On that day I received thirty papers that were a pleasure to read and that bespoke each author's pleasure in having written a paper whose inner workings and function had been firmly grasped.

In a similar manner, in the second week they processed the skill of descriptive writing through the four stages and six levels, and in subsequent weeks they worked through the other rhetorical models.

Notes

1. Benjamin Bloom, *Taxonomy of Educational Objectives: The Classification of Educational Goals,* Handbook 1, *Cognitive Domain* (New York: Longman, 1956).

2. Jean Piaget, *The Child and Reality* (New York: Grossman, 1973).

3. D. Phillips, "The Search for Mental Structures: Reality or Rhetoric," paper presented at the National Conference on Reasoning, Piaget, and Higher Education, Denver, April 1980. Dr. Phillips is at the University of Iowa, Iowa City.

2 Integrating the Curriculum

Letters and Literature

Dee C. Storey
University of Nebraska, Lincoln

In March 1980, the United States Postal Service celebrated letter writing by issuing a set of six commemorative stamps and attempted to encourage the return of the friendly letter. An elementary school might follow the same procedure and celebrate a week of letter writing to create a spirit of personal correspondence that will last throughout the year.

To bolster letter writing in fourth through sixth grades, several children's books can be employed. Many authors who include letters in their books stress a character's need for personal communication and a feeling for the importance of the received correspondence. In Irene Hunt's *Across Five Aprils*, the Civil War is raging and the distant families wait and worry about what has become of their loved ones.

> They lived through many dreary days of writing. Everyday someone . . . would drive into town to see if there was a letter. For many days there wasn't, and the only slim comfort they could find was to remember that there was one chance—one in a hundred. Then finally there came a letter from Ross Milton. . . . There were many letters from both Jenny and Ross Milton that summer, letters brought hope and comfort to the family at home.[1]

The letters became a source of solitude, sorrow, and joy. In days without mass media, the postal service linked distant family members and friends.

Letters about Letters in Literature

Colby Rodowsky, author of *P.S. Write Soon*, noted that she added a letter to each chapter because:

> Years ago when one of my daughters was about 11 or 12, a letter came to the house for her addressed in her own handwriting . . . When I asked her why she had written herself she said simply "I like to get mail!" This started me thinking about pen pals that some of

43

my children had—and how much this meant to all of us, and how much we all liked to get mail. (And I'm so glad you asked why I decided to write a book using letters rather than why I decided to write a book about handicapped which is what people usually ask— and is not where I started at all.)[2]

Sore Loser (1976), by Genevieve Gray, is totally comprised of letters, memos, notices, and the like. Sixth-grader Lauren, a new boy in town, writes to his friend from his old home town. Lauren pours out his emotions regarding not being able to adjust to his new surroundings and the people he meets. In regard to writing the book in this fashion, Gray commented:

> . . . the format was chosen more or less by accident. The theme reflects my own childhood, which was none too happy. Even as a very young child, I insisted to myself I must surely be a worthy human being even though it seemed that everyone about me saw me as conceited, selfish, and sullen. A nightmarish feeling, that. Lots of tear soaked pillows when no one, positively no one, believes in you. And then, magically, like the Ugly Duckling, to at last emerge!
>
> This was the idea I wanted to dramatize. After writing for a week and getting nowhere, I hit on the strategy of using *only* the bulletins, teachers' notes, etc., which I had already included in the manuscript. The story grew from that beginning.[3]

The letters add the personal touch needed to convey the emotional impact that a narrator might not be able to express. Lauren is a very real person and, although letters from his friend are not included, the reader can sense the great strength in the friendship the two boys share.

Susan Terris, author of *The Chicken Pox Papers*, comments on how her own experience is presented via ten-year-old Gussie, who comes down with chicken pox on her birthday and receives stationery for a gift.

> I used the letter format because that was the shape of my original idea. As I began, I thought I would tell the whole story through letters. When it became apparent that this approach was not going to work, I began on the narrative needed to add dimension to the characters and situations. I came up with the idea for the letters because I once fired off a series of them myself when I was sick on my birthday. Readers seem to love the letters; and they respond by writing me letters that sound as open and sassy as Gussie's.[4]

Authors have a variety of reasons for including personal correspondence in their writing; their methods for weaving the letters into the story vary as well. While their books and intentions differ, the authors all seem to emphasize the valid form of personal writing used in communication.

Literature Containing Letters

While there aren't many children's books revolving around personal correspondence, those titles that do emphasize correspondence encompass a wide range of expressed emotions. The presentation of letters usually occurs throughout the chapter; very few books are totally comprised of letters. Titles with personal correspondence include:

Daddy Long Legs by Jean Webster. Orphan Jerusha Abbot mysteriously receives a scholarship to attend college. To qualify for the funds she must write one letter a month to her benefactor, whom she dubs "Daddy Long Legs."

Letters to Horseface by F. N. Monjo. In fictional letters to his sister, fourteen-year-old Mozart describes his travels with his father, the people he meets, and the music he studies and writes.

Letters to Pauline by James Kruss. A series of letters, stories, and poems are exchanged between the author and Pauline, a friend from the author's former home.

The Mailbox Trick by Scott Corbett. Kerby receives a box of stationery for his birthday; he writes two poison-pen letters and a letter to the governor about being a good citizen.

P.S. Write Soon by Colby Rodowsky. Sixth-grader Tanner writes about imaginary events in letters to her pen pal Jessie Lee. Tanner feels her life is boring and everyone is unfair to her.

School with a Difference by Yvonne Meynier. During the German occupation of France during World War II, two sisters are sent to boarding school in the country. Family letters exchanged are based on actual experiences of the author.

Sore Loser by Genevieve Gray. Lauren moves to a new town and writes all about it to his friend Mark. Memos and letters from teachers and the principal describe Lauren as a square peg trying to fit into a round hole.

Toby Lived Here by Hilma Wolitzer. While Toby's mother is in the hospital recovering from a nervous breakdown, Toby is in a foster home. She writes to her mother and desperately awaits the return mail that should bring some comfort—but no letters ever arrive.

Yours Till Niagra Falls, Abby by Jane O'Connor. Abby goes off to summer camp without her best friend. She writes letters pleading to return home but finally settles down to liking camp. The letters show how a writer corresponds differently with a variety of people.

Other Books of Interest

Sesyle Joslin, in *Dear Dragon,* outlines several types of letters children may encounter. Joslin develops a situation requiring a letter and provides sample correspondence.

Manghanita Kampadoo's *Letters of Thanks* is devoted to the thank-you notes Lady Katherine Huntington sends to Lord Gilbert in response to gifts she receives during the Twelve Days of Christmas. Throughout this delightful parody, the letters express her sentiments.

The letters and notes described in Robert Kraske's *The Twelve Million Dollar Note* add mystery and suspense to the various forms of written communication. Kraske tells of notes and letters in bottles that are set afloat in oceans and rivers. Some letters are pleas for help, while others are basic greetings or messages from oceanographers using bottles to chart currents. The journeys and final outcomes of these notes make interesting reading.

Although Mercer Mayer's picture book *One Monster After Another* does not deal with seagoing messages, it is similar in some respect to the previous title. A letter is snatched from a postal carrier and is routed among a variety of monsters. The correspondence manages to fall in the clutches of a Letter-Eating Bombat, a Stamp-Collecting Trollust, a Paper-Munching Yalapappus, and a host of others before it is finally and dutifully delivered.

Points for Discussion

While teaching letter writing we often neglect the "whys" behind correspondence. We inform children about technicalities (headings, openings, bodies, closings) and forms (business, thank-you, and friendly), but we may not always create a desire for children to investigate the importance of written communication. The following questions might stimulate classroom discussion of letter writing.

1. How do letters effectively communicate the writer's intent?
2. What kind of letters get answers?
3. How do spelling, penmanship, and grammar have an impact on communications?
4. How do you write an interesting letter?
5. What changes can you bring about as a result of writing a letter?
6. Why write a letter when you can make a telephone call?
7. How do recipients of correspondence feel about letters? Why?
8. What kind of letters do you like to receive? Why?

9. What do you feel about letter writing? Why?

10. What is letter-writing etiquette and how does it influence correspondence?

Letter writing can be fun and informative if there is a purpose for it other than learning how to write a letter. Children, like adults, want a response when they write. Correspondence penned in English class should be aimed at receiving (1) information/material, (2) a reply to questions, or (3) printed proof of a letter being received. Students might write to other schools inquiring about the English curriculum, or they might write an open letter to the community explaining an English project they have been working on. Literary magazines for children (such as *Cricket*) might encourage "Letters to the Editor" in response to the contents of an issue.

Letters and literature go hand in hand in the English curriculum. The combination of the language arts is a way in which children can see theory put into practice. Communication is very much a part of the English class, but it also needs to be a part of the world outside school. Letters accomplish that goal.

Notes

1. Irene Hunt, *Across Five Aprils* (New York: Grosset & Dunlap, 1965), p. 156.

2. Based on personal correspondence from Colby Rodowsky, July 1, 1980, to July 31, 1980.

3. Based on personal correspondence from Genevieve Gray, July 1, 1980, to July 29, 1980.

4. Based on personal correspondence from Susan Terris, July 1, 1980, to September 2, 1980.

References

Carrock, Malcolm. *Tramp*. New York: Harper & Row, 1977.
Corbett, Scott. *The Mailbox Trick*. Boston: Little, Brown & Co., 1961.
Gordon, Sheila. *A Monster in the Mailbox*. New York: E. P. Dutton, 1978.
Gray, Genevieve. *Sore Loser*. Boston: Houghton Mifflin Co., 1976.
Hunt, Irene. *Across Five Aprils*. New York: Grosset & Dunlap, 1965.
Joslin, Sesyle. *Dear Dragon*. New York: Harcourt Brace Jovanovich, 1962.
Kampadoo, Manghanita. *Letters of Thanks*. New York: Simon & Schuster, 1969.
Kraske, Robert. *The Twelve Million Dollar Note: Strange But True Tales of Messages Found in Seagoing Bottles*. New York: Elsevier/Nelson Books, 1977.
Kruss, James. *Letters to Pauline*. New York: Atheneum, 1971.

Mayer, Mercer. *One Monster after Another.* Racine, Wis.: Golden Press, 1974.
Meynier, Yvonne. *School with a Difference.* Translated by Patricia Crampton. New York: Abelard-Schuman, 1964.
Monjo, F. N. *Letters to Horseface.* New York: Viking Press, 1975.
O'Connor, Jane. *Yours Till Niagra Falls, Abby.* New York: Hastings House, 1979.
Rodowsky, Colby. *P.S. Write Soon.* New York: Franklin Watts, 1977.
Terris, Susan. *The Chicken Pox Papers.* New York: Franklin Watts, 1976.
Webster, Jean. *Daddy Long Legs.* New York: Grosset & Dunlap, 1912.
Wolitzer, Hilma. *Toby Lived Here.* New York: Farrar, Straus & Giroux, 1978.

An Integrative Approach to Teaching Composition and Speech at the University Level

Kathie Webster, Patricia Van Dyke, Mary Lee Hummert, and
Rose Ann Wallace
Northwest Missouri State University, Maryville

While specialization has enabled educators to extend the limits of knowledge much farther than would have otherwise been possible, it has also affected our concept of education and has caused our disciplines to become more and more fragmented. Looking at college and university programs, we become aware that we "educate" students by exposing them to an arbitrary number of those fragments. We assume that at the end of the four years or one hundred twenty-four hours, or whatever the requirements happen to be, the student will understand the interrelationship of these fragments. Even though one program or division cannot hope to overcome totally the problem of fragmentation, colleagues in the fields of speech and composition have potential for reducing some of this fragmentation as follows: (1) by emphasizing common rhetorical elements in the two skill areas, (2) by capitalizing on the traditional general education format, in which basic speech and composition courses are required, and (3) by taking into account research findings that reveal the close relationship between the language skills.

First of all, speech and composition emphasize common principles of communication. For example, both deal with matters of stating a main idea, developing persuasive evidence, and organizing a coherent presentation of the parts of the speech or essay. In both composition and speech, a student is taught methods of presenting clear instructions, comparing two ideas, and changing an audience's mind through well-reasoned, well-developed argumentation. Finally, matters of style, audience, and editing either in spoken or in written communication are basic to both composition and speech courses. All of these common elements exist, yet the separation of the two courses results in their commonality going unappreciated by teacher and student.

Not only are the skills similar, but the importance of each course to a sound general education program is widely recognized. The problem for teachers of the two disciplines, however, is making the most of the time given to them for these skill areas. By team teaching the two courses, the common concerns of the two skill areas, in what is typically referred to as an integrated skills format, can benefit both the teachers and the students. In addition, the skills teachers can take into account research that demonstrates the overlap inherent in the two skills.

A number of studies in language testing theory point to the common factors underlying all language skills. For example, in the field of language pedagogy, Johansson found that the test scores of students on both their first and second language tests clustered together in factor analyses, indicating similarities of skills and commonalities across modes and even across languages.[1] In a study of freshman composition students' test scores on various language measures, Wallace found similar relationships among the types of language skills tested.[2]

Furthermore, teachers of rhetoric are beginning to be aware that the research and methods of speech communication teachers are valuable sources for teaching rhetorical principles in composition. In a recent review of resource books outside composition, Harrington named no fewer than twenty-five speech books that could assist composition teachers in planning their courses. According to Harrington,

> Rhetorical theory can be directly applied to both oral and written composition with only minor modifications to adjust for differences attributable to change of media. At least four areas of Speech Communication should be of special interest to the composition instructor: public speaking, argumentation and debate, persuasion, and rhetorical theory and criticism. Each of these areas has produced a literature too voluminous to be comprehensively reviewed.[3]

For reasons based on the similar and complementary nature of the skills taught, the correlations between the two established by test theorists, and the benefits to both teacher and student accruing to an integrated approach to general education, four teachers at Northwest Missouri State University, two from the Speech Department and two from the English Department, followed usual administrative and pedagogical procedure to design and establish an integrated skills approach. The administrative procedure was relatively uncomplicated. Since the students enrolled in two different classes and received two different grades the administrative relationship was internal: two sections of speech were merely combined with two sections of English composition. Both speech sections were scheduled for 10 o'clock and both English sections for 11 o'clock. A speech section and an English section were assigned to the same room, and the same students had to be enrolled in the corresponding sections of speech and English. In effect, this meant that a two-hour block was available for instruction three days a week. One class could meet for half an hour and the other for nearly an hour and a half as material and needs, rather than the clock, dictated.

The pedagogical procedures were equally uncomplicated. A month before the start of the fall semester, the two English instructors met with the two speech instructors to identify the instructional objectives for each course and match those that were similar and/or complementary. For example, the "English" goal of developing the students' skill in phrasing a central idea is complementary to the "speech" goal of developing the students' skill in phrasing a central idea. Both shared the objective of improving the students' ability to express ideas in clear, correct, and effective language.

After establishing pedagogical correspondences, they outlined the sequential structure of the courses. With the course outlines and matched objectives before them, they determined which objectives could be met simultaneously through joint assignments, which could be introduced first in one course, and reinforced through a later assignment in the other course, and which could be reached at the same time through different though related assignments.[4] Since both courses began with the analysis of communication, the instructors decided to handle this material through joint assignments and classroom experiences. This approach would give the students a clear picture of the interrelationships, similarities, and differences between spoken and written communication as well as a theoretical base for understanding the experimental course structure. The instructors planned a second joint assignment later in the course to teach the use of the library for research, a skill essential to both classes.

It was possible to reach only some course objectives through joint assignments since the sequence of teaching made it necessary to plan for a related skill to be taught earlier in one course than it would be in the other. For example, the composition instructors taught the narrowing of topics and construction of thesis statements early in the term, while the speech instructors wished to emphasize these skills later in the semester. Thus these techniques were taught early in the composition class and later restated and reinforced by the speech instructors when they helped students plan their informative speeches.

The third group of objectives outlined by the instructors involved those that could be reached simultaneously by the teachers' using different, but related, speech and composition assignments. For example, during the time that the speech instructors would be teaching interview techniques in preparation for an interview assignment on career choices, the composition teachers planned to make two related assignments: (1) to read and discuss three interviews from *Working* by Studs Terkel and (2) to interview a classmate using a structured set of questions and then write a paragraph drawing a conclusion about the person. Although the instructional objective of the composition teachers would be to practice supporting a thesis, their assignments would also support the instructional goal of the speech instructors.

As the semester progressed, the four teachers met frequently to adjust the plan based on their experiences in the courses. To insure coordination, the English instructors usually attended the speech classes and the speech teachers usually attended the English classes.

While numerous exercises and assignments were used, one set described here illustrates the tremendous potential possible with the integration. Using the Helen Puzzle, the Scrambled T Puzzle,[4] and the 3M Transparencies of Geometric Designs,[5] the instructors helped sensitize students to the problems inherent in giving and receiving information.

In each class, the English instructor presented a 3M transparency of an abstract design on the overhead projector and asked students to write instructions that would allow another individual to reproduce the figure. Students rather quickly produced their paragraphs and assumed that their descriptions were quite clear. The instructor then collected the descriptions, which were to be distributed to the other section later in the class. Meanwhile, the speech instructor followed the initial writing exercise using the Scrambled T Puzzle. The speech instructor asked students to find a partner and for each set of partners to sit back to back. One partner volunteered to be the teacher or explainer and the other to be the learner or follower. The instructor then showed the explainer how to complete the puzzle correctly and gave the learner an envelope containing enough pieces to reconstruct an identical puzzle. The explainer's task was to tell the learner how to assemble the puzzle. The learner's task was to listen carefully, following the instructions given and not to try to solve the puzzle independently.

After giving these directions, the instructor told the follower to remove the puzzle pieces from the envelope and the explainer to begin the instruction. Since they were seated back to back, neither could see the other's materials or actions. After explaining how to put the puzzle together, the explainer assumed the listener had assembled the pieces correctly. At this point, verbal feedback was permitted between the explainer and the follower. With the addition of feedback, the length of time necessary for explanation was greatly increased. The explainer began experiencing some of the frustration the listener had previously experienced and realized how difficult the sharing of a common meaning in communication actually is and how essential feedback is to the communication process. Once the puzzle had been completed, students discussed the communication concepts that were involved and formulated suggestions for giving directions.

Next the students received the descriptions written earlier by the other section and attempted to reproduce the original design. When the drawings were completed, they were returned to each writer. Since there were inaccuracies in the drawings, it was clear to the students that similar needs exist in both written and oral communication. In order to practice the principles they had discovered, the students repeated the oral and written exercises with much more satisfying results. The entire sequence of activities took place in one two-hour block of class time.

The puzzle and drawing/writing exercises are valuable in themselves since the students are able to understand the nature of the relationship between the speaker-writer and listener-reader after completing them. But the exercise and the discussion have other benefits: the rules derived by the students for giving clear instructions became the key to stating a thesis and providing good examples in the next writing assignment, the process paper. The pattern of combining the oral and written experiences established in the opening exercise continued throughout the semester.

Implications of Combining Oral and Written Communication

As a result of combining the two fields, students begin to learn that more than one application of experience exists. As students are shown similarities between oral and written communication, these similarities reinforce and emphasize each other. With increased emphasis, learning should be increased. In addition, this combination provides an excellent opportunity for demonstrating dissimilarities between the two fields. For example, feedback exists in both oral and written communication but functions quite differently in each. Students generally are not aware of this difference. Their attention must be focused on the necessity of responding to immediate audience feedback throughout their oral communication. The prepared speech is not a finished product prior to its delivery. During presentation, it must be dynamic, changing as a result of audience feedback. Because immediate feedback is not possible in the written message, even greater awareness and consideration of the audience by the writer is necessary.

In addition, students become more aware of the differences between the receptive skills of reading and listening. As students understand these differences, they can effectively respond with the appropriate structure and style of their messages. For example, considerably less redundancy is necessary in both structure and content for written messages than for spoken messages. When reading, one can glance back over the message.

However, when listening, one cannot replay what has been said; rather, the speaker must provide the repetition.

The chief implication of the study seems to be that the integrated skills course increases the resources of both the speech and English teachers. The learning aids, the methodology, the terminology, and the texts of another discipline can be brought to bear on an aspect of the communication process. Also, whenever teachers come together for the benefit of the students to work on a common problem, the fragmentation in the educational process is reduced for the teachers as well as for the students; as educators, we gain a renewed sense of our long-term goals.

Notes

1. S. Johansson, "Partial Dictation as a Test of Foreign Language Proficiency," in *Papers in Contrastive Linguistics and Language Testing,* eds. C. Schaar and J. Svartvik (Lund, Sweden: Lund Studies in English, 50, 1973), pp. 123–49.

2. Rose Ann Wallace, "Issues of Validity and Reliability in the Testing of Freshman Composition" (Diss., University of New Mexico, Albuquerque, 1978).

3. David Harrington, Phillip M. Keith, Charles W. Kneupper, Janice A. Tripp, and William F. Woods, "A Critical Survey of Resources for Teaching Rhetorical Invention," *College English* 40 (February 1979): 653.

4. Karen Kruper, *Communication Games* (New York: The Free Press, 1973), pp. 45–51.

5. "Transparencies of Geometric Designs," *Education Age Supplement* (Minneapolis: Minnesota Mining and Manufacturing Company, 1968).

Unifying the Language Arts Classroom: A Theory and a Strategy

Greg Larkin
Northern Arizona University

We have a penchant in U.S. education for strategies, methods, and techniques. The desire to improve our discipline is good, but if the individual improvements are not solidly based on a thoughtful and accurate perception of the larger issues, then new strategies are really just fads, modern methods merely gimmicks, and the latest techniques only futile panaceas. With this caveat, I would like to present a concrete strategy for successful classroom management of an English language arts class. But first, it is necessary to establish a brief theoretical framework on which to ground this strategy.

Unfortunately, the current practice in our profession seems to place at opposite poles the study of literature and the study of "practical" aspects of language, such as grammar or composition. In this bipolar world, there are two sorts of teachers—the Old Guard, who teach only literature regardless of the overt subject matter of the day, and the Assault Troops, who are currently expanding their professional horizons to include composition, grammar, and other "practical" and nonliterary uses of language. The Old Guard are grudgingly allowing the newcomers a small foothold in the profession, a "rear of the bus" position, while they themselves blithely drive on at the wheel of the great literary vehicle, steering a course straight to the land of literary criticism.

Meanwhile, at the back of the bus, a revolution is taking place that often appears designed to split the bus in half. In fact, some schools already boast departments of literature and departments of literacy—separate kingdoms where unity used to prevail. The same thing happened in earlier centuries—the total language department used to encompass the disciplines of classics, speech, drama, and linguistics. As an estate that is divided equally among all children of every generation loses its value, so the language arts are losing their value by the continual fragmentation taking place at every level.

This problem is not merely a theoretical construct of concern only to administrators. It pervades every language arts classroom. For instance, many teachers and students agree that grammar is a boring subject. If the teacher is foolish enough to try to teach it, immediately the whole class either falls asleep or starts playing around, neither of which is conducive to the learning of grammar. Most instruction in "practical" language arts suffers from the same lack of commitment and interest by both students and teachers.

Literature, on the other hand, is usually of interest and value to both teachers and students. The intensity of human values and human cultures in literature involves students actively in the learning process. But if language and its products do form one complete whole, is it really impossible to unify a literature lesson and a "practical" lesson in the same classroom? Are we doomed to watch the blessed rage for specialization devour our profession and spit it out as so many intricately subdivided but incompatible bits?

I would like to answer "no" to the above questions. There are no boring topics, only boring teachers. Furthermore, a dedicated teacher can use literature and grammar together in many ways to form the basis of a unified classroom experience. The teacher *can* break the dichotomy of "teaching literature" or "teaching practicality." Consider the following classroom exercise:

> Exercise 1. How many sentences can you make?
> This Is Just to Say
>
> I have eaten
> the plums
> that were in
> the icebox
>
> and which
> you were probably
> saving
> for breakfast
>
> Forgive me
> they were delicious
> so sweet
> and so cold

Here are the sentences one rather unimaginative student wrote in response to this poem by William Carlos Williams:

1. I have eaten the plums.

2. The plums were in the icebox.

3. You were probably saving the plums.

4. You were probably saving the plums for breakfast.

5. Forgive me.

6. They were so delicious.

7. They were so sweet.

8. They were so cold.

Obviously, many more sentences could be made.

In doing this exercise, even the unimaginative student experiences literature and grammar simultaneously and firsthand. The student experiences the concentrative powers of poetry firsthand, as well as the grammatical possibilities inherent in even a simple assertion.

The student can deepen both literary and grammatical experiences by combining members of the first group of sentences into various alternatives, such as:

> Exercise 2. Combine any pairs from Exercise 1.
>
> Examples:
>
> 1. The plums I have eaten were in the icebox.
> 2. The plums, which I have eaten, were in the icebox.
> 3. I have eaten the plums which were in the icebox.
> 4. The plums which were in the icebox were eaten by me.

Again, many more combinations are possible. The point is not to find the "right" combinations or even to find the best ones. What is important is that as the students compare the various possible versions among themselves, they are learning about grammar. For instance, numbers 1 and 2 illustrate the difference between restrictive and nonrestrictive clauses. Numbers 3 and 4 demonstrate the active and passive forms of the same assertion. Every combination has at least one practical lesson in it.

On the other hand, as the students compare the various possible versions against the original poem, they are learning about poetry. In Williams's poem the teacher of literature can discuss graphically, in the context of this exercise, such poetic principles as line length, line division, stanzas, punctuation, and rhythm. On a more intricate level, questions of imagery, juxtaposition, and point of view are all clearly brought to the students' attention by the contrasts between the poem and the various prose versions generated by the exercise.

There is no end to the grammatical and literary possibilities in just this one short poem. Consider:

> Exercise 3. Combine any three sentences from Exercise 1.
>
> Examples:
>
> 1. The plums were delicious, sweet, and cold.
> 2. Although you were probably saving the plums in the icebox, I have eaten them.

3. Forgive me for eating the plums which you were saving.

4. The delicious, sweet plums were in the icebox.

Let's take an example from Andrew Marvell's "To His Coy Mistress" to see if there really are "practical" lessons in every poem:

> Had we but world enough, and time,
> This coyness, lady, were no crime.

Of course this is not a whole poem, but grammatical and literary lessons on the subjunctive ("were"), the role of time ("time"), word order ("Had we"), vocabulary ("coyness"), and idiom ("no crime") are possible. These simultaneous lessons need not slight either the practical or the literary. To cite just one example in more detail, in the vocabulary lesson, the following questions would be good possibilities for simultaneous learning:

Exercise 4:

Practical	*Literary*
1. Define *coy*.	1. Has *coy* changed meaning since Marvell wrote?
2. What are the connotations of *coy*?	2. What other words in the poem pick up on the basic image of *coy*?
3. Use *coy* in your own sentence.	3. In the context of the whole poem, why did Marvell choose just the word *coy* instead of some other close synonym, such as *shy*?

Many other similar paired lists of questions could be devised for other practical-literary investigations into "To His Coy Mistress" or any other poem. More advanced "practical" principles such as organization or coherence can be investigated through poetry. Do poems have any of these qualities? If so, can the poems be used to teach the practical points and the practical points be used to teach the poems? The answer is "yes," as demonstrated in the following exercise based on "The Dance":

Exercise 5:

> In Breughel's great picture, The Kermess,
> the dancers go round, they go round and
> around, the squeal and the blare and the
> tweedle of bagpipes, a bugle and fiddles
> tipping their bellies (round as the thick-
> sided glasses whose wash they impound)
> their hips and their bellies off balance
> to turn them. Kicking and rolling about
> the Fair Grounds, swinging their butts, those

shanks must be sound to bear up under such
rollicking measures, prance as they dance
in Breughel's great picture, The Kermess.

The above poem contains only two sentences. Rewrite it as a
paragraph containing at least five sentences. Make sure that the five
sentences flow together as well as the poem does.

Can we talk about coherence in this poem without simultaneously
teaching poetry and organization? Is there any inherent difference between
at least some of the ways Williams holds this poem together and the way
a student uses transitions to tie together a freshman English theme? In
other words, to do this exercise with any skill at all, the composition
student must examine the coherence of Williams's poem and "translate" it
into prose inter- and intrasentential links. In so doing the student will
begin to gain a literary appreciation for Williams's poetic skill and a
practical ability to write coherent prose.

These poems by Sylvia Plath and William Wordsworth should generate
some literary-practical exercises:

Exercise 6:
I'm a riddle in nine syllables,
An elephant, a ponderous house,
A melon strolling on two tendrils.
O red fruit, ivory, fine timbers!
This loaf's big with its yeasty rising.
Money's new-minted in this fat purse.
I'm a means, a stage, a cow in calf.
I've eaten a bag of green apples,
Boarded the train there's no getting off.

     or

It is a beauteous evening, calm and free,
The holy time is quiet as a Nun
Breathless with adoration. . .

If you need some suggestions, try "abstract and concrete" or that
favorite commandment of composition teachers, "Use more detail." Soon
you should be able to select your own poems or your own "practical"
problems and to start generating your own material altogether. It's great
fun for both students and teachers—and it's great learning experience.

Two points crucial to the success of this approach are that (1) a
student's understanding of and appreciation for great literature should be
improved and enhanced, not inhibited, by the kinds of questions that a
teacher of grammar or composition might ask about the language in the
work of art and (2) a literature teacher can teach a stimulating lesson on
a nonliterary topic using great literature for the examples on which the
lesson is based. Literary artists do use language in "practical" ways.

But even more important than these two points is the conclusion that a good English teacher can combine the literary and the practical in one classroom experience. One need not be chosen over the other. In fact, as the literary and practical are combined imaginatively, the teaching and the learning of both are improved in ways that could not be duplicated were either studied in isolation, as is all too often the case in our language arts classrooms today.

Uses of the Commemorative Speech in Teaching Writing

Melvin H. Miller
University of Wisconsin, Milwaukee

For several thousand years, the basic formula for competence in language has been threefold: (1) studying precepts and principles, (2) thorough practice in writing and speaking, and (3) observing the practice of others. It is the third part of the formula that concerns us here. Teachers of writing may not realize that certain types of speeches—the commemorative speech in particular—offer rich resources in the uses of language. Such speeches, says Richard Murphy, "give us a microcosm of humanity, a man (or woman) in high thought and feeling, in a worthy cause, seeking by his word-artistry to make his audience care."[1]

Robert Burchfield, the chief editor of the Oxford dictionaries and a noted expert on the English language, said recently, "The two best disciplines for teaching young people to use language properly are speaking in public and perpetually practicing writing in a formal way."[2] Burchfield recognizes the significance of the oral mode in writing and the usefulness of understanding the directness, the simplicity, the impressiveness that can occur when a speaker and an audience sense that they have business together. To study such speeches is to set higher goals for performance in both writing and speaking.

The following procedure can be used successfully in a language arts class to help students understand such speeches and to appreciate how speaking, writing, reading, and listening are interwoven into the fabric of effective language.

If you ask your class what specific speeches they remember, you are not likely to get many answers. But in almost every group someone will mention the Gettysburg Address or Martin Luther King's "I Have a Dream" or perhaps John F. Kennedy's Inaugural Address. Some students may remember their parents mentioning Franklin Roosevelt's First Inaugural Address or Douglas MacArthur's Speech to Congress. You may be surprised to learn that every speech mentioned will almost surely be one we consider as ceremonial—one in which the speaker speaks *for* the group, one designed to inspire and to help men and women see beyond themselves.

This is a useful point at which to start. Why do we remember these speeches rather than others? What causes a speech to have a life beyond the moment of delivery? A class ought to be able to determine that speeches that deal with universal themes live on because they are not only timely but timeless. A careful study of such a speech can reveal to the student how the components of language come together—audience, sender, message, and occasion at some important moment in time. Studying a speech instead of an essay has the additional value of language being used in a real life situation where choices have to be made and constraints considered and where, in the best of such speeches, noble theme and noble language unite in ways that not only help us remember but enoble us as well.

One of the serendipitous aspects of studying such speeches is that gaining a full understanding of the situation as well as the speech is a fascinating way to study history. To understand Pericles's Funeral Oration is to understand Athens in the fifth century B.C., to understand King's "I Have a Dream" is to understand the beginnings of the civil rights movement in this country. To understand Winston Churchill's "Blood, Toil, Tears, and Sweat" is to understand how brave words and little else held a desperate England together in the dark days of 1940.

The following steps outline a classroom procedure that works at the high school or college level in utilizing such speeches.

1. Choose a fairly short speech but one that is well enough known so that material about the speech will be readily available.

2. If possible, duplicate the speech and provide enough references so that the student can become familiar with the period.

3. Ask the student to read the speech and the background material and to write a one-page commentary on *one* aspect of the speech. Taking only one point forces the student to be specific and avoids both generalities and a "book report" approach. Tell the student the report should talk about "why," "how," and "to what end," rather than being a report on what was said. Areas applicable to all speeches include: organization, language, situation, setting, mood, purpose, use of supporting materials, and theme.

4. Have the student read the paper in class. The varieties of approach should provide for lively discussion and a better understanding of the many factors involved.

Let's take an example. Suppose you were to use Pericles's Funeral Oration as a commemorative speech to study. Since it has lasted 2500 years, it is a good example of a significant theme that is both timely and timeless. It is short and easy to understand, and it is well within the capability of a high school student. It includes some memorable examples of language used supremely well. Here are some suggested questions for a one-page commentary:

1. What was the setting for the speech?
2. Who was Pericles?
3. What was Athens like at this time?
4. Compare Athens and Sparta as places to live.
5. What role did Thucydides play in this speech?
6. How did Pericles adapt to the occasion?
7. What happened after the speech?
8. Which portions of the speech could be given today? Why?

Here are some other choices:

Winston Churchill, "Blood, Toil, Tears, and Sweat." This famous speech was given in the House of Commons on May 13, 1940. It was the first statement made by Churchill as prime minister. If nothing else, students can learn that Churchill asked four things of the British people, not just "Blood, Sweat, and Tears."

Martin Luther King, Jr., "I Have a Dream." This widely known and widely available speech, delivered August 28, 1963, suggests the power of language. Rich in metaphor and with a tone poem quality of rhythm and parallelism, it ought to be listened to as well as read.[3] Interesting questions concern the mood of the day, the problem of speaking to a crowd of 200,000, the status of civil rights at the time, the crowd reaction, and the effects of the speech.

Senator Michael J. Mansfield, "Eulogy to John Fitzgerald Kennedy." Of all the thousands of eulogies delivered at the time of the assassination of President Kennedy, none is more moving or more sensitive than this eloquent tribute, which in eight paragraphs shows how powerful language can be when used well. It was delivered in the rotunda of the Capitol, Washington, D.C., November 24, 1963.

There are many source books for these speeches and numerous other speeches. The reference books listed are just a few of the available collections. As Murphy says, "It is a pity not to draw freely upon this heritage."[4]

Notes

1. Richard Murphy, "The Speech as Literary Genre," *Quarterly Journal of Speech* 44 (1958): 127.
2. Richard Murphy, "A Conversation with Robert Burchfield," *U.S. News and World Report* (December 15, 1980): 71.
3. Recorded versions of the speech are available under the titles *We Shall Overcome* (Folkways 5592) and *Great American Speeches*, volume 3 (Caedmon Records, TC 2035).
4. Murphy, "The Speech as Literary Genre," p. 127.

References

Aly, Bower, and Aly, Luciel F. *American Short Speeches.* New York: Macmillan Co., 1968. For those seeking short speeches, this is a useful source of twenty speeches, including Lincoln's Gettysburg Address, Churchill's "Blood, Toil, Tears, and Sweat," and John F. Kennedy's "Ich bin ein Berliner."

Aly, Bower, and Aly, Luciel F. *Speeches in English.* New York: Random House, 1968. This collection includes Roosevelt's First Inaugural Address, Churchill's Address to Congress, MacArthur's Speech to Congress, and Kennedy's Inaugural Address, with additional commentary on the speeches.

Hibbitt, George W. *The Dolphine Book of Speeches.* New York: Doubleday, 1965. Nearly sixty speeches are reproduced by speakers ranging from Socrates to Goldwater. Commemorative speeches include Pericles's Funeral Oration, Lincoln's Gettysburg Address, Mansfield's Eulogy to Kennedy, King's "I Have a Dream," and Churchill's "Blood, Toil, Tears, and Sweat."

Linkugel, Wil A., Allen, R. R., and Johannesen, Richard L. *Contemporary American Speeches,* 4th ed. Dubuque, Iowa: Kendall-Hunt, 1978. Your library may have one of the four editions of this collection, each of which contains about forty speeches. Four commemorative speeches have appeared in all four editions: King's "Love, Law, and Civil Disobedience," MacArthur's "Farewell to the Cadets," Kennedy's Inaugural Address, and King's "I Have a Dream."

Matson, Floyd W., ed. *Voices of Crisis: Vital Speeches on Contemporary Issues.* New York: Odyssey, 1967. This is a collection of twenty-seven speeches on modern significant themes, including a number of ceremonial addresses.

Peterson, Houston, ed. *A Treasury of the World's Great Speeches.* New York: Simon & Schuster, 1965. This paperback is the granddaddy of one-volume speech collections. It includes 278 speeches by 230 speakers ranging from Pericles to Malcolm X.

3 Structuring the Writing Assignment

Steppingstones to Success: A Journal-Based Composition Course

Dawn M. Wilson
Kent State University

Many composition teachers ask students to keep journals, usually defining the journal as a repository for significant thoughts and observations, but rarely making any connection between writing done in the journal and writing done for a grade. In this vein, Robert Herrick refers to the journal as a "record of growth, thinking, and daydreaming"[1] without mentioning any relationship that journal writing might have to course content. As such, the journal is a valid supplemental assignment: it provides students with writing practice, it gives students an opportunity to react to and comment on class discussion, and it offers students a chance to explore ideas and feelings. But the journal can be more than an isolated entity. Journal writing can be an integral part of the college composition course, useful in developing students' writing abilities and in providing them with an understanding of the writing process. I consider journal writing a skill-building, confidence-inspiring activity that can be a steppingstone to success on regular theme assignments.

My version of journal keeping combines freedom with practicality—some entries are free choice; others are designed to give students an opportunity to rehearse their ideas before becoming committed to them in themes. Each week, students write two free choice and two assigned entries. Every other week, a theme is due. Each theme must have some basis in a journal entry. As a result, students explore several possibilities before settling on a topic; thus, they are unlikely to choose an unworkable subject.

Helping students progress from journal entry to theme through in-class work that focuses on the processes involved in composing is an essential part of this program. At the beginning of each class session, students—working alone or in pairs—are assigned journal tasks. At the beginning of a semester, I use activities such as "isolate the 'center of gravity' of a given entry," "discern places to add or delete material," "detect ways to reorganize the entry."[2] Later, when students have mastered the larger scope, I move to finer points. I begin class with journal activities designed to develop specific skills needed to write themes. Students are asked to read through their entries for different purposes on different days: to add details, to improve word choice, to change sentence structure, to provide transitions, to invent material, or to construct more effective leads. So that students understand that this kind of work needs to be done on every assignment, such activities need to be repeated throughout the course.

I require students to submit journal entries with final drafts so that I can diagnose where their writing may have lost direction. Many times, for instance, students have not reorganized their original attempts when a more effective arrangement of ideas is clearly necessary. Other times, students have padded their themes with irrelevant material instead of attempting to stay with the journal idea and adding examples and details that support it. By checking the theme against its origin in a journal entry, I can offer insights useful to students when they revise.

At the end of the semester, the entire journal is given a grade based largely on effort. Since journal entries are done prior to the rough-draft stage in writing, they cannot be graded in the same way that themes would be assessed. Mechanics and syntactic maturity are not useful measures for evaluating journals. Specific criteria that I do use as guidelines for a holistic assessment of a student's journal include

1. a wide range of topics and ideas,
2. the ability to focus on a narrowed topic in some entries,
3. the use of concrete details and specific examples throughout,
4. sufficient personal involvement in most entries to demonstrate reaction to and reflection about experience, and
5. completion of assignments.

This kind of directed journal writing leads students toward proficiency in discrete writing skills. For instance, students who are expected to use concrete detail in their journal entries are more likely to use abundant detail in their themes; students who are asked to focus on their topic in some journal entries will be ready to write effective thesis sentences for their themes; and, most importantly, students who write journal entries before themes inevitably become involved in some revision and are prevented from submitting rough drafts as final copy.

Paramount to a journal-based composition program is the sequence of journal assignments, which becomes, in effect, the sequence for the entire course. What succession of rhetorical modes best approximates the way students learn? What is the best developmental sequence? The answers to these questions vary greatly. James Britton feels that "expressive" writing is a "pivotal point from which other modes can be differentiated."[3] What he means is that since students write more effectively when they are writing for themselves, to clarify an idea or to express a feeling, they should be given many opportunities to write expressively before they are asked to assimilate the skills needed for more public prose. Similarly, James Moffett defines the sequential path as "a growth scale going from the personal to the impersonal, from low to high abstraction, from undifferentiated to finely differentiated modes of discourse."[4] James McCrimmon advocates a "cumulative sequence" beginning with "specification and descriptive writing, moving to comparison-contrast and classification, and concluding with persuasion."[5] Donald Murray's primary concern, however, is that the sequence of skills be based on the practice of experienced writers, stressing those recursive steps taken naturally and automatically by competent writers.[6] Combining the essence of these views, after using preliminary free-writing exercises as icebreakers I move from personal writing to narrative writing (following Britton's and Moffett's suggestions); then, I move to more traditional forms (using McCrimmon's idea of sequence). Throughout (as Murray recommends), I supplement these assignments with in-class journal activities, such as those already mentioned, which offer insights into the composing process by leading students through different steps in writing as they progress from journal entry to theme.

Journal writing can help students in different ways at different stages of a composition course. In the beginning, when students are apprehensive about writing, casual journal assignments (such as "If I had a million dollars . . ." or "If I could go anywhere in the world . . .") tend to make writing interesting and nonthreatening.[7] At this stage, journal writing encourages students to get ideas down on paper. And since journal entries are not graded for mechanical flaws, students have the freedom to write quickly and comfortably. As Donald Hall observes:

> It is essential . . . that daily writing not be corrected. In order to clear the passageway, in order to provide that freedom that will develop the muscles of writing, the student must scribble away without worrying that anyone is looking over his shoulder.[8]

Thoughts do not have to go unsaid because the struggle to express them accurately was insurmountable.

Since it is important to continue the level of comfort that has been developed through initial journal entries, I assign some form of personal writing for the first theme. Of all the rhetorical modes students will study, personal writing is the closest to journal writing. Also, since students enjoy writing about their experiences, personal writing is the least demanding while still teaching skills that will be valuable later. As students write about their experiences, either in narrative or essay form, they learn to stay with the story line and not to stray into irrelevancies; as they determine the point of their narratives, they are learning to generalize.

Descriptive writing comes next in my program, though some might choose to begin with it inasmuch as specificity is vital to all writing. But descriptive writing is more difficult for students to control than personal writing—selecting an appropriate word to capture a sensory image is a demanding task. A strictly logical developmental sequence must give way to a sequence based on the level of difficulty for students.

When I move to expository and persuasive writing, I first ask students to respond in their journals to topics that represent all the rhetorical patterns of organization to be covered: comparison-contrast, definition, classification, cause-effect. I give selected journal assignments from each category, any of which could later be expanded into themes. Then I introduce students to the concept of invention. As Frank D'Angelo defines it, "In its broadest sense, invention is any mental activity that will bring to conscious awareness something previously unknown."[9] Until this point, the mere act of responding to a set of journal topics is sufficient for students to discover an abundance of material; further, subjects for personal and descriptive writing often have a built-in organizational pattern. But since more structure is required in expository and argumentative essays, it is essential that a topic be carefully considered before it is selected for a theme. A set of directed "probe" questions or "heuristics" can lead writers into previously unexplored areas of their subjects, coaxing forth supplementary material and suggesting methods of development. By recording responses in their journals to such questions as "What are its parts?" and "In what respect is it like or unlike something else?"[10] students soon acquire a store of information from which thesis sentences emerge. An added benefit of this procedure is that students can choose, from many possibilities, the topic best suited to a given rhetorical pattern—subject finds form rather than form dictating subject.

Throughout the course, I stress the distinction between process and product—between journal entry and theme. So that students do not ever get the idea that a good journal entry is equivalent to a good paragraph or theme, I explain and illustrate the differences. In Linda Flower's terms, journal entries are examples of writer-based prose, while themes and paragraphs are reader-based.[11] Or, as Elaine Maimon puts it, journal entries, being akin to rough drafts, are like talking to family or friends, whereas formal writing is like talking to strangers.[12] Journals illustrate the kind of cognitive processing that results in process writing, while themes and paragraphs should be thought of as products. Journal entries can take the reader along through the discovery process as an idea is being formulated; themes and paragraphs should synthesize main points first and should be organized according to carefully thought-out plans.

The process of writing a journal entry, then, is different from the process of writing a theme. Writing a journal entry involves transcribing thoughts and ideas almost as quickly as they occur, a process that generates material. Finishing a theme involves recasting, shaping, and editing.

Students need instruction in transforming a journal entry into a theme. In the beginning, too much direction in completing the product—the theme—may be counterproductive. Students cannot possibly understand the entire composing process at the outset. At some point, however, students appreciate explanations of how to invent more material, how to reorganize and rearrange existing ideas, and how to detect stylistic weaknesses. Also, students must realize that they have to throw out any material that is not related to the main idea. Thus, when students select the journal entries that they would like to use as the basis for their theme assignment, the first step is to isolate the main point. Students might be told to write a one-sentence statement of purpose based on the focal point in the journal entry. Next, students may benefit by listing in brainstorming fashion the details that come to mind once the central issue has been determined. After this, some more writer-based prose is in order to clarify the topic and to elaborate on it. Heuristic procedures may be helpful here. When enough material has been generated, the students should again read over their journal passages, underlining parts that are significant. More list making may be necessary before the next steps: outlining, deciding what the thesis will be, and determining the topic sentences for the individual paragraphs. Finally, it is time for the rough draft.

Since journal entries are assumed to be unfinished, students show an increased willingness to change them substantially as they rework them. Rather than the superficial changes students make when they revise traditional themes (which are often no more carefully written than journal entries), students who revise journal entries do indeed recast and reshape their material. We should not expect the beginning paragraphs and themes to have been revised as extensively as the later ones will be, of course. The early essays will be similar to the journal entries in which they are based. But our goal should always be in sight. We should expect final essays to have been transformed. As Mina Shaughnessy puts it, final essays should give "various signs of having been wrought—that is, of the writers' having intervened in deliberate ways to change their wording or to correct errors."[13] This willingness to change what has been written is crucial.

Students benefit from as much writing practice as they can possibly get. Donald Hall maintains that the most valuable part of a good English course is daily writing practice.[14] A journal-based composition program provides this additional practice while at the same time helping students become competent, proficient writers.

Notes

1. Robert Herrick, "Discovering the Journal," *Teaching English in the Two-Year College* 2 (1976): 92.

2. Peter Elbow, *Writing Without Teachers* (New York: Oxford University Press, 1973).

3. James Britton, *The Development of Writing Abilities: 11–18* (London: Schools Council Publication, 1975), p. 163.

4. James Moffett, *A Student-Centered Language Arts Curriculum, Grades K–13* (New York: Houghton Mifflin Co., 1968), p. 371.

5. James McCrimmon, "A Cumulative Sequence in Composition," *English Journal* 55 (April 1966): 426.

6. Donald Murray, *A Writer Teaches Writing* (Boston: Houghton Mifflin Co., 1968).

7. Ken Macrorie, *Telling Writing* (Rochelle Park, N.J.: Hayden Book Co., 1970). The book provides excellent ideas for anyone using either free writing or journal writing in a composition course.

8. Donald Hall, *Teaching Writing Well,* 3rd ed. (Boston: Little, Brown & Co., 1979), p. x.

9. Frank D'Angelo, *Process and Thought in Composition* (New York: Prentice Hall, 1980), p. 31.

10. Ibid.

11. Linda Flower, "Writer-Based Prose: A Cognitive Basis for Problems in Writing," *College English* 41 (September 1979): 19–20.

12. Elaine Maimon, "Talking to Strangers," *College Composition and Communication* 30 (December 1979): 367.

13. Mina Shaughnessy, *Errors and Expectations* (New York: Oxford University Press, 1977), p. 276.

14. Hall, p. x.

Structuring for Composition

Sharon Feaster
Northeast Texas Writing Project, Kilgore

Structuring for classroom management means that teachers have a plan and a purpose in mind for each activity. Students (and teachers) are more likely to stay at a task if they know where they're headed. In composition, the strategy involves using the complete composition process, choosing whatever activities will accomplish the purpose.

Structure is defined as "made up of interdependent parts." For composition assignments, these parts are four stages of the composing process: prewrite, write, rewrite, and postwrite. Assignments can and should be based on these four stages. Each stage should be considered with every assignment that is made. Sometimes one stage receives most of the emphasis in an assignment; sometimes teachers may decide to skip a stage—but this should be a conscious decision, not one due to forgetfulness.

This does not mean that every instance of student writing should be structured and analyzed so completely. Carefully structuring free writing and journal writing would defeat the purpose of writing to generate ideas and to develop fluency and a love for words. It would be incorrect to suggest this procedure for "long" assignments; some very helpful writing assignments can also be very short, while some long assignments are given just to take up time or convince someone in authority that teachers are doing a good job.

There should be a purpose for every instance of writing. Teachers should be concerned with process instead of just product. One way for teachers to stress process is to structure assignments on the stages of the composing process so that practice will be quality practice.

The first stage of the composing process is prewrite—getting ready to write. In the secondary school, often the preparation for writing is "Read the story and write a summary (or answer the questions)." While reading a story and then writing a response is an acceptable assignment, there are many other ways of prewriting. Prewriting includes, but is not limited to showing a film as preparation for sequencing,

showing a film without sound as preparation for story writing,

listening to music for mood and tone,

role playing for dialogue,

brainstorming for classification,

playing a related game,

flying a paper airplane for process description,

going outside and observing for description,

reading a comic strip for learning to use quotations,

visiting a cemetery before reading and discussing death,

seeing the movie before reading the play or book,

giving a pretest to determine starting point for instruction,

drawing a picture for description,

looking at a painting for point of view,

discussing personal experiences before reading,

petting an animal or using a "feely bag" for description.

The second stage is write—putting ideas down on paper. This stage currently receives the most emphasis. An assignment such as "Write a five-page report on anything you want" will usually merit a rough draft, with students grinding out their prose, sentence by painful sentence. However, this can be one of the easiest of the four stages. Once prewriting has generated ideas, they flow rapidly from mind to paper. Free and loop writing can be a part of prewriting as well as part of the first draft of the writing stage.

The rewrite stage is where the sweat (and sometimes tears) comes in. Students take the written composition and restructure it for coherence, unity, and organization. Can sentences be eliminated or expanded or combined? Can paragraphs be rearranged to make better sense? Is the reasoning logical? Do word choices set the right tone? Is the piece appropriate for the intended audience? And finally, students must get out the dictionary and the handbook and check out all the mechanical and grammatical aspects.

The last stage is postwrite—what to do with writing when it's finished. Sometimes this means turning it in to the teacher for a grade. More often, it means reading it to peers (small or large groups or to a younger class in school. During a session on letter writing, it means writing a letter to a real person and then mailing the letter. Postwrite means publishing writing in a class or school or community newspaper. It means taking it home for parents to read. It means doing whatever possible to provide an audience other than the teacher. This gives purpose to writing. We all write better and are more concerned with our writing when we know that someone else will read it.

Structuring an assignment involves sitting down and planning. A suggested format that provides planning for all parts of the process includes:

Purpose of Assignment

How Long We'll Spend on It

Description of Assignment

Preparation I Need to Do (including materials, resources, etc.)

Stages (indicate what's involved in each)

Prewrite

Write

Rewrite

Postwrite

Some sample assignments using this format follow. The emphasis in the first assignment is on prewriting, or getting ready to write description by practicing brainstorming and classification.

Purpose. Develop skills in description and classification

How long. One to two periods

Description. Students will generate a list of characteristics through brainstorming and then will categorize the characteristics into classes provided by the teacher.

Preparation. Bring sheets of butcher paper, felt marking pens, several spring flowers.

Prewriting stage. Ask students to look at the spring flowers (pass them around and smell and touch them) and talk about other flowers they see. Have them look out the window and talk about other things they see in the spring. Get them to imagine things they see, smell, touch, taste, and hear in the spring. In small groups, have students brainstorm and write down things that are related to spring. They may write single words or phrases. Use felt markers and butcher paper. Students may draw some simple illustrations, if desired. Put the charts around the walls. Read them and talk about the five categories of the senses. Make a list on the chalkboard of all the words or ideas related to each sensory category.

Writing stage. Have students in small groups pick the category they would like to write about. Then have students compose a paragraph on the sense they chose, using words and phrases from the board (to prevent copying misspelled words from the charts). Have each student contribute one sentence.

Rewriting stage. Have students discuss in which order they would like to put their ideas. Number sentences in order. Exchange rough drafts with another group, which will read to see that all sentences belong to the sensory classification the group chose. Have them read secondly for organization. The original authors listen to the response group's ideas and decide what to do about a final draft. After the paragraph has been written in order, the authors read for mechanical and grammatical errors. They may ask another group or person to read for this purpose also. (This assignment assumes that students have been taught how to work in response groups.)

Postwriting stage. Tape the finished paragraph on top of the original brainstorming chart for each group. Have someone in each group read the paragraph to the class.

Purpose. Practice in describing feelings

How long. One period

Description. Students will listen to a piece of music and then describe the feelings aroused by the music.

Preparation. Bring appropriate music ("Grand Canyon Suite," "Danse Macabre," etc.), record or tape player.

Prewriting stage. Tell the students to listen carefully to a piece of music, keeping aware of the feelings it evokes. Play the music (or a portion of it) without giving the title or any explanation.

Writing stage. Ask students to write phrases or sentences that describe how they felt as they listened. Ask them to tell which sounds in the music made them feel that way.

Rewriting stage. You may choose not to ask them to rewrite or polish this assignment.

Postwriting stage. Ask the students to tell their basic emotion in one word. Have students who used the same basic word get into groups to read their phrases or sentences to each other and discuss why they reacted that way. Another option would be to divide students into unlike groups and have them discuss their differences.

Another version of the previous assignment could be:

Prewriting stage. Have the students listen to music, then have them draw what the music makes them think of.

Writing stage. Ask students to describe their picture and tell what in the music made them imagine what they drew.

Rewriting stage. Have students read their papers and show their drawings to the response group. Ask each group member to respond positively, telling how the author successfully combined the mood of the music with the picture and writing. The author considers what the group members said and produces a finished copy of the paragraph.

Postwriting stage. Display the pictures and paragraphs together. If you like, post them separately and have students read the paragraphs and decide which pictures they go with.

This assignment teaches students how to use quotations and dialogue and prepares them for writing dialogue of their own (a future assignment).

Purpose. Instruction in writing and punctuating dialogue

How long. One to two periods

Description. Students will use comic strips to transfer words in the balloons to written dialogue.

Preparation. Prepare transparencies of comic strips and a ditto with a comic strip; bring enough Sunday comic strips to go around, either individually or in small groups.

Prewriting stage. The day before, ask students to bring in copies of comic strips and comic books. Look them over briefly and use the overhead projector and chalkboard to demonstrate how cartoonists indicate words spoken by their characters. Demonstrate on the overhead projector by putting quotation marks around the words in each balloon and then transferring the words to a sentence in paragraph form. Demonstrate indenting for each different speaker and the necessity for adding, "Hagar said," or "Archie shouted" to explain who's doing the talking. Pass out a ditto with a comic strip containing two speaking characters. Have students first put quotation marks around words in each balloon and then transfer the conversation to their papers. Explain again the necessity for adding words to indicate who's speaking. Show them the correct model on the overhead.

Writing stage. Pass out new comic strips, either to individuals or partners, and have the students put in quotation marks and transfer the dialogue to paper. Remind them about adding words to indicate who's speaking.

Rewriting stage. Partners exchange papers with another set of partners to see if they understood the dialogue, if they indented with each change of speaker, and if they used quotation marks correctly. Editors may also look at the explanatory words and compare them with the cartoon to see if the authors have caught the mood. They may suggest some substitutes for "said" that will fit the cartoon better.

Postwriting stage. Partners read both of their dialogues before the class; each takes a part and makes sure that intonation is used to get the meaning across.

Here's an assignment for writing description:

Purpose. Practice in describing

How long. Two to three periods

Description. Students will spend time observing and making notes on what they see, hear, feel, taste, or smell; next they will write a descriptive paper of three to five paragraphs in length.

Preparation. Choose an especially descriptive passage to read to the students. Cut a two-yard length of string for each student. Students will need to go outside.

Prewriting stage. Read a descriptive passage to students. Explain to them that they will take their piece of string outside, make a circle on the ground with it, and sit (or stand) in their circle. This is "their" place of property for fifteen minutes. They are to make notes (or free write) on what they observe. They may write about what they observe on the ground within their circle or what they observe from the vantage point of their circle.

Writing stage. After making notes or free writing for fifteen minutes, students return to their class and write for fifteen minutes on what they have observed, using their notes or free writing.

Rewriting stage. Each student writes a second draft, reorganizing the paper as necessary. You may discuss classification if necessary. Once students have decided how to organize their thoughts, they read to see if they've kept to their plan. Have them exchange papers with a partner, who will read to detect the organization pattern. Partners meet and discuss ideas with each other. Each editor comments on the vividness of the writer's description.

Postwriting stage. Post the papers around the room. Artistic students may want to draw a picture to go with their description.

These are just a few examples of ways composition assignments can be structured to provide freedom to learn and write. To make the assignments even more effective, you should participate in each exercise with the students, then share your writing. Students will learn from hearing and seeing how you handled the assignment.

Second-Grade Authors Provide the Structure for Their Writing Success

Joyce L. Parent
Boothbay Writing Project, Boothbay, Maine

Julie is eight years old. As of April of this school year, she has written and illustrated twenty-eight books.

Stacy, another second grader, is writing to a raisin company. She had read a story with her reading group about raisins. During a discussion of the story, several questions were raised that weren't answered in the textbook, and she is writing the letter to obtain the answers to these questions. When she can't spell *raisin* she consults her friend Mark, who responds by asking, "Where do you think you could find the word?" Stacy remembers that it would be in the reading book; she looks up the correct spelling there.

Her classmate Jed is writing about World War II. He has obtained a lot of information from his grandfather, a veteran, and has written a section concerning his grandfather's involvement. To continue, Jed needs further information. He goes to the school library and signs out three texts on the war to use as additional resources in his research.

Selena is writing a book about animals. When the pages in her booklet are full and she still has more to say, she removes the staples holding the pages together. She gets more paper, adds it to the sheets she has filled, restaples the booklet, and continues writing.

Billy and Joe are writing, seated at the same table. Joe is working on a letter of inquiry to an orange grower. Joe says, "Billy, how does this sound?" He reads the piece aloud as Billy follows with his eyes on the paper. Billy comments, "I heard your voice stop someplace in here." He points at a line. Joe asks, "Where?" Billy replies, "Read it again and see." Joe does; he locates the end of a sentence and in so doing is self-editing the piece for punctuation and capitalization.

Lying on the floor, her piece of writing fastened to a clip-board, Alison is reading a section aloud to her classmate, Aundrea. There is a great deal of expression in her voice as she reads, "My father once saw a lady who had purple hair because she dyed it!" Her teacher, as an observer, asks, "Alison, do you know how to show someone else who might read this piece that you want it to be read with the expression you are using?" Her forehead furrows and her head cocks to one side in puzzlement, so the teacher goes on. "You can use a mark at the end of the sentence called an exclamation point, instead of a period. It looks like this." The teacher makes the mark. "Oh, yeah! I've seen those in our reading books. That's how we know to make our voices sound excited when we read out loud."

During the exchange with Alison, there is another observer—Jamie. He is working on a book about hornets. A few moments later, he asks the teacher to listen to what he has written. When he reaches a sentence that says, "Boy, did it hurt!" he proudly points to the end of the sentence where *he* has prominently placed an exclamation point.

This is typical of what has been taking place in my second-grade classroom this year. As participants in the Boothbay Writing Project under the directorship of Nancie Atwell, thirteen colleagues and I, teachers of grades one through eight, are learning that *students* provide the structure for their success in writing when teachers function as responders and advisors, not as assigners and correctors. This project was designed using a model based on the 1978–80 research findings of Donald Graves, Lucy Calkins, and Susan Sowers in their NIE-funded study of young children's writing abilities.

For one hour each day, Monday through Thursday, the children in my classroom—and, on occasion, their teacher—are involved in the various stages of composing: rehearsing or prewriting, drafting, revising, editing, and rewriting.

Students choose whatever materials they need to produce a completed piece of writing. Tools and paper for writing are provided in abundance: crayons, colored pens, pencils, and markers; wide-lined paper, narrow-lined paper, unlined paper, construction paper, and sheets of the various kinds of paper stapled together to make booklets of assorted sizes.

In addition, students choose the particular place or position in which they will write. They can be observed sitting, standing, or lying in any available spot in the room, moving from one place or position to another as their needs and purposes as writers dictate. They also choose their own consultants—the human and printed resources that will assist them in gathering and reformulating their ideas and information. Choices of topics, purposes, and audiences are made entirely at the discretion of these writers as well. They write about things that interest *them*: subjects about which they have some degree of knowledge or want to learn more.

Because this class of second graders has the freedom to be responsible for all of the options available to the writer, they control their own learning. Because there is an intrinsic purpose for writing on whatever topic they select, a desire to write has been created.

The purpose for which many are writing is publication; the satisfaction of seeing one's efforts printed in some form is an essential factor in their motivation. Their compositions have been published as collaborative books to which each student has contributed a story, or individual books that one child alone has authored. Stories and poems have been submitted to the school magazine, and their articles have been printed in the local newspaper. Bulletin board displays of the students' writing have been arranged both within the classroom and outside of it in corridors, in view of a larger audience.

The anticipation of receiving responses to pieces they have written also provides motivation to these young writers. This may be seen in the variety of letters of inquiry they've addressed to different manufacturers, and in their personal letters written to friends and relatives. But response to writing isn't limited to comments about finished pieces. When a writer seeks help during the drafting stages of a piece, that response comes in the form of questions that allow the author to reflect on the content of the piece and, again, to make choices:

How did you come up with this topic?

Who is your audience for this piece?

Would this part be clear to the audience?

Do you need to say this again (in cases of repetition)?

Would you be willing to delete (or change) this?

Is there anyone else you'd like to read this to who might be helpful?

What do you think of this piece?

What parts need more work?

What do you want to do next with this piece?

Having internalized a sense of audience, each writer knows that a composition is finished only when it is free of errors. When the writer decides the content of a piece is set, he or she then self-edits, sometimes seeking the help of a classmate in this process. Then a final conference is held; at this time the teacher serves as a responder to the writer's questions and concerns about the mechanics of the piece. Some typical questions second-grade writers ask about their writing are:

Did I spell *tangerine* right?

Would you show me the marks I need that shows this person is talking?

Is this how you abbreviate *road*? Capital *R-d*-period?

Do I need apostrophe *s* when I write, "The *cat's* dish was empty?"

When all the questions the writer has about spelling and usage have been asked, then the teacher becomes an editor, pointing out any remaining errors. The child holds the correcting pen or marker and changes anything necessary, so that the individual writer is still in control of what is happening with the piece. With teacher questions similar to the following, the piece is edited and finalized:

Is there anything you think may not be spelled correctly?

Is this an asking or telling sentence? What stop punctuation do you need?

You used a period at the end of this sentence; what can you tell me about the first letter of the next word?

Isn't *Scott* a name? What should be at the beginning of it?

Melanie wants to send a copy of a story she has written to her grandparents; she asks that a photocopy be made. "But," she states, "I don't want all these corrections I made to show." She is told that a photocopy would look exactly like the original and is asked if there is anything she might do to make a copy the way she wants it to look. "Sure, I could get another piece of paper and write it over; no one will know where I made corrections." She immediately heads for the paper supply, takes what she needs, and begins recopying the piece.

Similarly, Billy is busily recopying a story he worked on for three days. His teacher asks why he is doing this. "I want to put it up on the bulletin board for everyone to read," he answers. "I don't want to put it up all messy. No one will be able to understand it, and they won't want to read it."

No one had to tell these young writers that this step should be taken. Their awareness of audience prompted them to engage in rewriting and proofreading because they understand and readily acknowledge the need for doing so.

The results of conducting a language arts program in this manner have been most encouraging. The basic skills of writing are being internalized and applied, with at least a 90 percent accuracy rate in second graders' spelling, capitalization, and punctuation. It is the most successful program I have ever conducted, and its success lies in the fact that *I* am not conducting it; nineteen seven- and eight-year-old authors are.

Reference

Graves, Donald; Calkins, Lucy; and Sowers, Susan, "How Children Change in the Composing Process." Results of this 1978–80 study funded by the National Institute on Education are available from the University of New Hampshire Writing Process Laboratory.

The Waiting Game: Structuring the English Class for Prewriting

Barbara King
Douglass College, Rutgers University

In the not-so-distant days when teaching writing was product-oriented, teachers believed that all students could complete a writing assignment in exactly the same way and exactly the same time. Today, however, as the teaching of writing becomes more process-oriented, teachers realize that not everyone can complete a fully developed essay in forty-five minutes. In fact, students who can write their best in forty-five minutes are extremely rare. For this reason, teachers need to structure their classes to allow for differences in the writing process.

One way to do this is to recognize the need to allow time for a prewriting stage. Researchers such as Janet Emig and Donald Murray have emphasized the importance of a prewriting period. Prewriting activities do more than just keep students busy while they're waiting to write. These activities promote good writing by allowing students to explore their topics before writing the paper. Prewriting also helps students experiencing writer's block to overcome their fear of writing and their negative attitudes toward writing.

Allowing time for student differences in prewriting does not mean, however, that teachers should not assign deadlines. Deadlines are realistic and necessary. There must be some point when generating ideas ends and drafting the paper begins. The length of the prewriting period varies depending upon the writing assignment. Prewriting periods can vary from ten minutes to two or more class periods. A research paper, for example, has a longer prewriting period than a short descriptive paragraph. In either case, both the purpose of the prewriting period and the deadline must be made clear when assigning the paper.

Because the prewriting period varies from individual to individual and from assignment to assignment, some teachers find that allowing class time for prewriting is difficult. In a class of twenty-five students, for example, some will immediately start jotting down ideas while others stare at a blank page. Students who are having difficulty "getting going" and who "can't think of anything to write" do not have to sit there and wait for inspiration. There are a number of prewriting activities that teachers can offer students to help them become active participants in the "waiting game." These activities may be done as a class, in small groups, or by individuals. Moreover, students can be working on different prewriting activities within the same class. The following are some prewriting activities I have found successful in the classroom.

Writing is the most frequently used prewriting activity. Journals have become very popular in English classes from grade school through college and can be used in a number of ways during prewriting. Since the audience for journal writing is the self, students can use journals for free writing to warm up before writing a paper. They can also use their journals for brainstorming a specific topic. Using free writing to brainstorm often helps to clear the writers' minds and to help them focus on the assignment. This free writing also may be done in student notebooks or on single sheets of paper. The important thing about free writing is that it is not to be handed in to the teacher. One form of focused free writing for a paper on a favorite movie, for example, might include having students make lists of movies they have seen recently.

Talking is a natural form of prewriting that is often overlooked in the classroom. Encouraging students to talk as a class, in small groups, or one-to-one can help them if they are grasping for something to say. Talking can be helpful for the class provided the students follow the ground rule to "keep it down." A small group may begin the writing assignment on "My Favorite Movie" by talking about movies they liked or didn't like. While talking, students often recall facts and details that they had forgotten.

Questioning is a prewriting activity that can include writing and talking. When students are assigned a topic or when they decide upon a topic of their choice, they can explore the topic by jotting down questions that they would ask about it. These questions can be written in their journals or on papers to share with others in the class. One variation on writing questions is to have students ask them aloud while they are meeting in small groups. These questions often follow the five *w*'s and *h* of journalistic reporting: Who? What? When? Where? Why? How? For the favorite-movie assignment, students might ask the following: Who were the stars? What was the message or theme of the movie? Where did the story take place? When was the film made? How effective was the photography? Why did you like the movie? How did the main characters change or develop?

Reading can be another important prewriting activity. Using prewriting time to read books, newspapers, magazines, or other students' papers can offer students new ideas and new points of view. In the example of the favorite-movie assignment, students might spend part of their prewriting time reading movie reviews in magazines and newspapers.

Researching is a form of prewriting that enables students to gather specific information they wish to incorporate into their papers. For my example, "My Favorite Movie," students could go to the library or resource center to research some old film they've recently seen on television. In this case, part of their prewriting may be reading and note taking—a form of prewriting that professional writers frequently use. If the school has a media center, researching may include viewing films or slides on the art of film.

Acting can be an effective form of prewriting. Like talking, acting can involve the class as a whole, small groups, or individuals. Some students find that enacting ideas or incidents helps them focus more clearly on a theme. Teachers can provide limited or extensive creative dramatics activities for these students. If the whole class is willing to participate, these dramatic exercises can be done in the classroom. If a group or individual wishes to explore acting as prewriting, the exercises can be done in a library conference room, in an empty classroom, or in the auditorium. An acting exercise for the paper on a favorite movie could include students enacting a climactic scene from the movie. The students may, if they wish, share this with the class as a whole.

Doing something else can also help students to prepare to write. If it is a day when absolutely nothing seems to work for some students—they've tried free writing and nothing has developed—it may be helpful to have them do something totally different for a while. The amount of time depends, of course, upon the deadline. They may need time when, to borrow Peter Elbow's metaphor, their thoughts have to sit on the back burner and cook slowly. Doing something else may include outside reading assignments, worksheets, vocabulary exercises, or another writing assignment that needs rewriting. Doing something else may be something physical such as cleaning the boards or straightening the files. It is surprising how doing something unrelated will suddenly spark an idea for the writing assignment that students were "stuck on."

These suggested prewriting activities are ones I have found successful with students from eighth grade through college. Other teachers can choose from them and add to them according to their students' interests. For most students these prewriting activities are less threatening than facing a blank page. Students feel more comfortable about writing because they can warm up to it, explore their topics, and write when they have something to say. This has a positive effect on their attitudes toward writing.

Structuring the English class to accommodate these prewriting activities means assigning deadlines that allow for a period of prewriting, recognizing that students can be working on different prewriting activities during the same period, and allowing students to choose the prewriting activity that best suits their needs. By structuring the English class to let students know these prewriting activities are available and acceptable, teachers will not only be answering the question "What do students do while waiting to write?" but also will be helping students understand the writing process. This, in turn, will lead to better student papers.

References

Elbow, Peter. *Writing Without Teachers.* New York: Oxford University Press, 1973.

Emig, Janet. *The Composing Process of Twelfth Graders.* Urbana, Ill.: NCTE, 1971.

Murray, Donald. "Write Before Writing." *College Composition and Communication* 24 (December 1978): 375–78.

Teaching Creative Business Letters and Memos

Joan T. Knapp
University of Colorado, Boulder

We who teach writing know that all writing is creative, but on a scale of one to ten, most of us would place business correspondence near the "one" level of creativity. Yet we know how crucial well-written letters and memos will be to the future careers of our students once they leave college. The problem we face is how to engage our students' imagination so that they will learn to write these apparently humdrum assignments effectively.

My solution to this problem is a series of individual assignments arranged in sequences. Assignments are typed on 3 × 5 cards and distributed to students, who then write their responses on transparencies with felt-tip pens. When these responses are projected, students realize each response is an incident in a sequence that tells a story of a hero who is rewarded for creative thinking and writing in a business situation. In theory, this exercise may sound too facile to be effective; in practice, if a teacher is creative enough to write assignments that tell a believable story, students become sufficiently involved, both as writers and as critics, to lift the exercise from the humdrum to the imaginative level.

In this article, the procedure for the exercise is presented in the form of a manual addressed to the teacher. The procedure is divided into five steps: designing the assignments, distributing assignment cards, arranging for responses, exhibiting and critiquing responses, and arranging for class evaluation.

1. Designing the assignments. Choose a situation immediately or potentially interesting to your students, design a sequence of assignments around it, and type these on 3 × 5 cards, adding labels and numbers. Here is an example of a sequence dealing with employment that I wrote for students at Colorado School of Mines:

Employment Sequence No. 1
You are Hopeful Engineer, a senior student at CSM, and you were interviewed two days ago by J.J. Employer, Personnel Director of Amoco Oil in Denver. Write a follow-up letter to Mr. Employer

thanking him for the interview and expressing your enthusiasm about the prospect of working for Amoco.

Employment Sequence No. 2

You are J.J. Employer, Personnel Director of Amoco Oil in Denver. Of the ten engineering students you interviewed for a job last week, only one, Hopeful Engineer of CSM, wrote a follow-up letter thanking you for the interview. Mr. Engineer also has excellent academic credentials. Write him a letter accepting him for the job and telling him why you have chosen him.

Employment Sequence No. 3

You are Hopeful Engineer, a student at CSM, and you have been offered a job by J.J. Employer, Personnel Director of Amoco Oil in Denver. However, Upstart Oil in Cheyenne has also offered you a job that not only pays more but will give you more field experience, which you want. Write a tactful letter to Mr. Employer explaining why you have accepted Upstart's offer and telling him that you may be interested in working for Amoco at some future time.

Employment Sequence No. 4

You are Hopeful Engineer, a student at CSM, and you have been offered a job by Upstart Oil in Cheyenne. Write a letter to M.M. Upstart, President, accepting the job and asking when you should report for work.

Employment Sequence No. 5

You are M.M. Upstart, President of Upstart Oil in Cheyenne, and you have received a letter from Hopeful Engineer, a student at CSM, accepting your job offer. Since you made the offer, however, your producing wells have run dry and your access to the new area you were planning to explore has been blocked by a lawsuit. Write Mr. Engineer telling him of your altered circumstances and explaining that although you are committed to your offer, you may have no work for him to do and no money to pay him. Suggest that he might be happier in another job.

Employment Sequence No. 6

You are Hopeful Engineer, a student at CSM, and you have just received a letter from Upstart Oil in Cheyenne telling you that, due to reverses in the company's financial position, the job that they offered and you accepted is no longer open. You were also offered a job by J.J. Employer, Personnel Director of Amoco Oil in Denver, but you declined this offer. Write Mr. Employer explaining what has happened and asking whether his job is still open.

Employment Sequence No. 7

You are J.J. Employer, Personnel Director of Amoco Oil in Denver, and you have received a letter from Hopeful Engineer, a student at CSM, asking whether the job he had declined is still open. Write Mr. Engineer telling him that although that job has been filled, there is a new opening that will involve more field work. Tell Mr. Engineer that this job is his if he wants it.

Employment Sequence No. 8
You are Hopeful Engineer, a student at CSM, and you have just
received a letter from J.J. Employer, Personnel Director of Amoco
Oil in Denver, offering you a job involving considerable field work,
which is exactly what you want. Since you had previously declined
an offer from Amoco in favor of another offer that fell through, you
are grateful for a second chance. Write Mr. Employer an enthusiastic
letter of acceptance.

In this sequence, it is Hopeful's gracious letter of decline to Amoco
that makes him comfortable in contacting J. J. Employer again. Looking
back at that assignment (No. 3), one can see that Hopeful must make a
choice here. Should he mention Upstart's offer of a higher salary or only
the chance for more field experience? Since only the responses are shared
with all class members, their perception of Hopeful's motive if he men-
tions salary is that he is jockeying for more money. Writers thus learn
that the "meaning" of their letters depends not on the intention of the
writer but rather on the perception of the reader.

Other sequences I have designed for CSM students include Irate
Customer's quarrel with the telephone company about a call to Bangla-
desh, Helpless Student's complaint against Greedy Landlord for refusing
to return a damage deposit, Safety Engineer's thoughtful handling of an
OSHA directive requiring employees to wear safety shoes, and Hotdog
Skier's success in persuading the Saloman Company to replace defective
bindings. The possibilities are limitless, but since prior developments must
be recapitulated on each card, I have found that an eight-card sequence is
maximum both for comprehension of the later assignments and for the
space available on a 3 × 5 card.

Designing assignments is by far the most demanding step of the
exercise. Other steps consume considerable class time but demand little of
the teacher.

2. Distributing assignment cards. Assignment cards are shuffled and
dealt, written side down, to the class. Each sequence must be fully dealt,
so it is advisable to have two or three short sequences so that you have
exactly the number of assignments for the number of students.

3. Arranging responses. I find that senior classes are capable of
immediate response, but freshman classes prefer to copy the card and
write a response out of class. In both cases, students write on transparencies with washable felt-tip pens, and I project these with the overhead. Students do not sign their names, and anonymity is further
protected by the pseudonyms provided in the assignments. Despite such
anonymity, I have found that students who are unembarrassed to turn in
"D" work to me will make a real effort to improve when they know their
work will be scrutinized by the class.

4. Exhibiting and Critiquing Responses. Next to the writing itself, class critique is the most valuable part of this exercise. I suggest that you not read the assignments; let the responses alone carry the story line. As responses are projected, ask students to put themselves on the receiving end and tell you what they understand the situation to be from each communication. When facts have been established, ask for several opinions about the appropriateness and effectiveness of the communication. Most writers are amazed to discover that their letters or memos sound abrupt, condescending, wordy, gushy, or confused to readers. The class will usually have plenty of suggestions for improvement, and these provide a good basis for discussion. When a solution has been agreed on, write it on the transparency with a red pen. Finally, ask for criticisms of sentence structure, spelling, punctuation, and letter or memo form, and make these corrections also with a red pen. All this takes time, but a fifty-minute period is usually sufficient for the projection of a seven- or eight-card sequence.

5. Arranging for class evaluation. This step is optional, but it provides a chance for input from the less vocal members of the class and also provides a basis for grading. Slips of paper are passed out at the beginning of the session and students are asked to grade each letter or memo in three categories—clarity, effectiveness, and accuracy—on a scale of one to five and also to specify a letter grade. I've found that while students are ruthless critics, they are generous graders, and the tally usually yields a higher grade than I would have given.

Thus, an exercise in business correspondence not only can be imaginative in the writing phase and instructive in the critiquing phase, but it can have a happy ending as well.

Causal, Not Casual: An Advance Organizer for Cause-and-Effect Compositions

Terry Dean
University of California, Davis

For many college students, particularly freshmen, cause-and-effect relationships pose problems. To begin with, the word *causal* is perceived and understood as *casual*, a mistake often reflected in the level of analysis in the composition itself. Students who manipulate causal relationships reasonably well in their everyday lives become bogged down when asked to write a causal paper. Many students have had little if any formal instruction in analyzing causal relationships and, when confronted by college assignments, have no idea where to begin. I have tried to minimize this confusion and bridge the gap between past experience and college assignments by using what David Ausubel calls an advance organizer.[1]

Simply stated, an advance organizer defines and gives examples of the unique characteristics of whatever concept you are teaching, and relates this concept to past, present, and even future experience of the student. The organizer provides an intellectual framework upon which to hang the specific details and problems the student will encounter when reading or writing a cause-and-effect essay. At each step in the presentation of the organizer, the general concept is clearly defined and explained, and it is related continually to the student's past experience. The process is not an inductive one where the student alone must discover the relationship; instead, everything is laid out as clearly as possible. The assumption is not that students do not know how to manipulate cause-and-effect relationships; their past experience shows they can. The teacher's job is to make connections between this past experience and the present situation where the student is having difficulty.

This article is an account of the steps involved in presenting the organizer. I try to relate the general concept not only to the composition as a whole, but to the paragraph and sentence as well. To begin, write three pairs of sentences on the board. The sentences that work best are

Reprinted by permission from *Exercise Exchange* (Fall 1981).

those that interest the class personally in some way. They should be fun to analyze.

1. Francisco ran out of gas. His gas gauge broke.
2. Venetia got an A on her midterm. She studied hard.
3. Veda smiled. Mark asked her for a date.

Ask students to copy the sentences and to identify the elements in the causal relationship. Have them mark a *C* over the cause and an *E* over the effect. The first two examples pose few problems, but the third is interesting because it can go either way. Next, ask students what words could be used to indicate the cause-and-effect relationship between the two elements. Put as many words as possible on the board. These will be used later to work with causal relationships on the sentence level. Write two more sentences on the board.

4. Billy Martin was fired.
5. Billy Carter stopped drinking beer.

Ask students to copy the sentences. Have them write an effect for number 4 and a cause for number 5, joining the sentence they write to the given sentence with an appropriate connector word. Have the students share with the class the various sentences they have written.

Once students can identify the elements in a causal relationship, ask them to define both *cause* and *effect*. If the answers are on target, put them on the board. If not, keep probing. A slightly wrong definition is preferable to no definition. The goal of this discussion is to show that cause and effect are defined in terms of one another. Having the students check their own definitions with those in the dictionary is a good way to demonstrate this point. When students realize that a cause and an effect are connected, you can focus on the strength of that connection and introduce the concept of degrees of causality.

I introduce this concept by listing the appropriate adjectives, verb forms, and adverbs that can be used to indicate the various degrees of causality.

necessary	will	always
probable	should	almost always
possible	could	sometimes
unlikely	shouldn't	seldom
no way	won't	never

The example I use to test for degrees of causality is "What produces good gas mileage?" The causes most frequently mentioned are good maintenance, proper driving habits, favorable driving conditions, and driving an economy car. Using the words on the list, see if you can determine the strength of the causal connection in each case and determine which causes are the most significant. You can go back to the first three sentences you put on the board and make the distinction between single and multiple causes. This distinction should be stressed because many students fail to consider alternative causes in college writing. In fact, I make a distinction between multiple causes that go back in time and those that exist at the same moment in time. One can explore the possibility at this point of tracing causal relationships from the present moment back to the beginnings of the universe. Nothing is more fascinating than trying to establish historical connections that relate to you personally, and nothing is more difficult than trying to demonstrate the validity of those connections.

Instead of going back endlessly, multiple causal relationships also exist at the same moment in time. Almost any current event that students are familiar with can be used. Here are some causes my students came up with to explain the events at Jonestown:

fear

force

racism

idealism

brainwashing

economics

For multiple relationships going back in time and those existing at the same time, analyze the degree of causality in each instance and make distinctions between the more significant and the less significant causes. By identifying and defining the elements in a causal relationship, by testing the strength of the relationship, and by distinguishing between single and multiple causes, you have presented the main characteristics of a cause-and-effect relationship that would be required for most papers. Once students understand these basic concepts, you are ready to make connections between their past, present, and future experiences. In each case call attention to the source of the data used to establish the strength of the causal connection; the difference between the source of data used in past experience and that used in college accounts for many of the problems students have with causal analysis.

To make students aware of how pervasive cause-and-effect relationships are, I ask them to recall the earliest time in their lives when they initiated an action in order to bring about a specific result. Since children learn very early to manipulate parents, students can usually remember an instance when they were five to seven years old, and sometimes earlier. In each case, test the strength of the causal connection and identify the source of data used to verify it. In all of these situations, the data come from personal experiences that are remembered.

A useful example of a causal relationship in the present is "What causes good grades?" If students say that studying causes good grades, test to see if that is a necessary cause. Provided that you have some knowledge of study techniques, you can combine causal analysis with some study skills review. Once you have a list of causes on the board, see if you can decide which are the most significant and which need to be defined more precisely. As you can see from the following list developed in class, it does not take long to discover the complexity that cause-and-effect relationships can have.

Causes of good grades:

IQ (what is IQ?)

study time

attending class

eating right

enthusiasm

motivation (different from enthusiasm?)

Again, most of the data used to test the strength of the causal connections will come from personal experience, although some students may have additional data from articles they have read on study techniques.

For cause-and-effect relationships that students will encounter in future college courses, I use actual examples from midterm and final exam questions. One midterm for a history class asked students to analyze how class, sex, race, and ethnicity affected the work options available to working-class women in the late nineteenth century. A psychology exam asked students to examine the validity of the hypothesis that people with an extra Y chromosome had a tendency toward violent behavior. Ask students how they would go about testing the strength of the causal connections in these instances. Then compare the cause-and-effect relationships in these college assignments with those in the students' earlier experiences. Is the nature of the relationship any different? Are the causes or the effects any more or less complicated? If you discuss these questions long enough, it will become clear that cause-and-effect relationships on the college level may or may not be more complex, but the real difference is the source of data used to prove or disprove the relationships. Students are not dealing with data from personal experience as much as dealing with secondary sources, data from reports and books, data that first must be well assimilated before students can deal effectively with the causal relationship. This means learning and internalizing the required data to the point where they become almost as familiar as personal experience. For students who believe that they are ready to write about an article or chapter if they have read it once, this will introduce the idea of mastering the material before attempting to test the causal relationships.

It is also useful to challenge the concept of causal relationships that has been presented by examining situations that seem to have the qualities of a causal relationship but that are flawed in some way. The lists of logical fallacies that most rhetoric books contain can be useful, but it is better to make students aware that in order to establish valid causal relationships, they need to ask questions and demonstrate the answers they come up with. Being able to question and prove the strength of a causal connection will be more useful in writing than simply recognizing a *post hoc ergo propter hoc* relationship.

The presentation thus far takes thirty to forty minutes, depending on how freely you let the class participate. In order to change the pace at this point, I have students work on sentence level cause-and-effect relationships using the connector words written down at the beginning of class. I supply them with some information and have them make up the rest on their own using some cause-and-effect patterns as a guide:

1. Make up an active voice sentence. Call this sentence X. Finish the sentence using this pattern: *X/because Y.*
2. Jerry Brown gives a speech = X. Complete the pattern *Whenever X/Y.*
3. I graduate from college = X. Complete the pattern *Provided that X/Y.*
4. A doctor discovers a cure for cancer = X. Complete the pattern *X/therefore Y.*
5. Women may be drafted = X. Complete the pattern *Because X/Y.*

An alternative to this exercise would be to have students perform a sentence-combining exercise that contained causal relationships.[2]

1. Our problems are solved.
2. Calvin chairs the program himself.
3. Calvin keeps his word.
4. Calvin finds someone to chair the program.

For the remainder of the class period students can write a short essay analyzing a causal relationship containing at least three causes. As an alternative to writing an essay, they could read a causal essay outside class and discuss the causal relationships in the essay. This could be followed up the next class period with an in-class essay based on the outside reading.

The advantage of the organizer is that it clearly defines the elements and steps in the process of causal analysis and allows students to recognize where they need work. For many people it is a tool for working in unfamiliar terrain. By pointing out similarities and differences in past, present, and future experiences, the organizer provides a bridge between the known and the unknown and helps to eliminate the *casual* from causal analysis.

Notes

1. Paul D. Eggen, Donald P. Kauchak, and Robert J. Harder, *Strategies for Teachers: Information Processing Models in the Classroom* (Englewood Cliffs, N.J.: Prentice Hall, 1979), pp. 258–308.

2. The following sentences and the causal patterns are from Willis L. Pitkin, Jr., whose approach to sentence combining emphasizes different binary relationships, in this case cause and effect, and is particularly useful because it can be used to reinforce basic thought processes on all levels of writing: essay, paragraph, and sentence. See his article, "X/Y: Some Basic Strategies of Discourse," *College English* 38 (March 1977): 660–72.

Constructing Composition Assignments

Sara Reimer Farley
Wichita State University

Most students I teach have, at the beginning of their first semester in freshman composition, no sense of the process of writing. Their concern is primarily the product. And since the product seems so distant and the barriers that separate students from the product so many, students cringe when an assignment is announced, crying immediately, "What do you want? Where do I begin?" If the answer is noncommittal (a repeat of the assignment) or nonexistent (the teacher having announced the assignment on the way out the door), the students often will procrastinate and finally rush through one draft the night before it is due, hoping that this time they have figured out what the assignment really called for.

I have tried various ways of stemming the tide of disappointment that swells from teacher and students alike at the various stages of the process (formulation, submission, evaluation, and return of the paper). I have had students work through the process on the board, edit other students' work, edit their own work, and completely rewrite, carefully following the directions I have scribbled in the margins of the unsatisfactory papers. Sometimes these strategies work—for the one paper. But give the students another assignment, and they flounder again. The problem arises during the process of writing and is especially evident in the product; the solution is found, however, in the framing or structuring of the assignment.

To respond appropriately and confidently to an assignment, students must have a purpose for writing, a real audience to write for, specifications of the task—its limits, conditions, possibilities, and, therefore, the basis for evaluation—and a recognition of the process of writing. The assignment, if carefully constructed, can provide this. It can provide cues to guide students through the entire writing process, allowing choices yet directing students to successful expressions of their aims.

Purpose in an assignment, whether the assignment stems from a reading selection or is chosen to illustrate a mode of development, must be stated so students see a *need* to write. This purpose must be established first, for as James L. Kinneavy asserts in *A Theory of Discourse,* "The aim of a discourse determines everything else in the process of discourse."[1] Although the purpose of an essay like narration or comparison might seem readily apparent to the instructor, the students need to hear or see the aim of the assignment so that they can begin consciously to choose their tone, language, and examples to meet that purpose. Admittedly, identifying the purpose of a piece of discourse will not automatically remove all obstacles student writers face. But without having a purpose, students will produce mere ramblings of thought, some of which by chance alone may come close to the expectations of the teacher. Assignments, then, must do more than state the mode of development. The assignment that I give for a narration essay states the mode of development and the purpose. The assignment is given after I have read a poem entitled "Ceremony," which is from the novel *Ceremony* by Leslie Silko, a Laguna Pueblo writer. Two lines of the poem establish the tone of the assignment: "You don't have anything/ if you don't have the stories."[2] The assignment is in two parts—a statement of condition and purpose and some cues for content:

> In the Indian culture, words—whether spoken or written—are considered powerful and sacred. In fact, the word is powerful enough to change reality. Such is the attitude we will have for this assignment. Your story should have greater significance than "We went skiing in Colorado" or "Our side won." You will be trying to particularize an event, to recreate it, to provide an illusion of reality. And in the retelling of that event, you will be introducing us (this class) to something we haven't experienced or suggesting a new dimension to something we have experienced.
>
> Remember a time when your view of a situation or yourself changed because of something someone said or did (or didn't say or do) or when your view of yourself contrasted with the way people treated you. Write a story about this event.

This assignment gives the students a reason to write: they are often intrigued with the power Indians accorded the story, and they remember a similar situation that they wish to externalize.

Furthermore, this assignment also establishes the audience. Knowing the audience is crucial for any writer. And knowing the make-up of the audience along with the purpose for writing helps the students assume an appropriate voice or stance. I have found it useful to establish the class as the audience.[3] Most of the students have trouble perceiving what an audience needs to know because the idea of an audience requires them to look outside of themselves. If that audience can be made real to them and if they can get immediate feedback by testing out a sentence, paragraph, or plot, these writers will be more conscious of what needs to be explained when they are separated from their audience. The audience should not be limited to one group. This is one variable that the teacher should be aware of and should use to increase the students' writing abilities.

The narration assignment given previously also begins to specify—for the students and the teacher—limits, conditions, and possibilities of the assignment. This specification answers the question, "What do you want?" by providing cues for content, organization, and skills to be demonstrated. The limits and conditions are important because students can begin measuring the success of their writing before the teacher evaluates their work. The possibilities are also important because students respond with greater enthusiasm if they have some choice in the assignment. Specifying the task enables the teacher to teach something about writing, to make connections between class discussions and the writing, or even to create class discussions. Once the work is turned in for evaluation, the teacher again uses these specifications to measure the students' work objectively based on the skills or techniques stated in the assignment.

The framing of assignments should not stop here, for the concentration is on product. If we want our students to value the writing process, then we should direct their energies in that direction. Therefore, in constructing assignments, I try to establish some specific ways for students to begin and to find a handle on their subjects. Prewriting tasks may begin with intuitive methods (like brainstorming) or intellectual methods (like particle-wave-field) or a combination of both. By specifying steps, I can help students figure out where to begin and also how to check their writing against the expectations of the assignment. An assignment for classification, for example, might be as follows:

> Letters to the editor have protested students' behavior—the vocal insults especially—during the spring festival productions put on primarily by the Greeks. The writers have complained that the attitudes of these dissenting students should not be tolerated and that some form of discipline should be administered so that the prejudices of these few students will no longer sully the motives of the civic-minded students. (Remember that all proceeds from the festival go to charity.) You feel a response is justified because you think the students need a broader understanding of types of insults, attitudes, dissent, discipline, prejudice, or motives. Write a letter to the editor in which you explain your position by classifying one of the terms.
>
> 1. To begin, select one of the terms and use it for your class (e.g., discipline), or take a subunit of the larger subject and use it for your class (e.g., self-discipline).
>
> 2. To arrive at subunits, make a list of the different ways the word can be used. Letters, for example, may be the alphabet, pieces of correspondence, among other things.

3. A purpose of classification is to discover a productive way of viewing an idea. For the subject you have chosen, try to come up with several different principles of classification, therefore discovering various groupings of the items in the class. Choose the principle that seems to be the most profitable for the situation.

4. Once you have decided on a principle of classification, jot down the categories that would result. You might also note examples of the categories.

5. Experiment with a thesis statement: it should identify the class and the principle of classification.

6. Determine the most effective order for arranging your categories.

7. The letter will be written in class. You may bring your notes.

This assignment establishes purpose and audience, specifies the task, and outlines the writing process.

Although the writing process tends to be recursive rather than linear, as this particular assignment might suggest, my students have found such assignments helpful because the process is broken down into more manageable units. The steps provide a guide through the process for students who are unsure of how to proceed. For students who have established their own patterns of writing, the steps can also serve as a reminder of areas to check if the paper does not seem to go anywhere. Of course, assignments given later in the semester need not be as detailed. Once students use some prewriting activities on their own, the teacher can drop specific instructions.

Constructing good composition assignments requires time and imagination of the teacher. But time spent in this endeavor will result in success for both the students and the teacher.

Notes

1. James L. Kinneavy, *A Theory of Discourse* (New York: W. W. Norton & Co., 1971), p. 48.

2. Leslie Silko, *Ceremony* (New York: Viking Press, 1977), p. 2.

3. James Moffett discusses the validity of the class as audience in *Teaching the Universe of Discourse* (Boston: Houghton Mifflin Co., 1968), pp. 193–98.

Helping Students Generalize, Specify, Clarify: A Sequence for Writing Assignments

Margot K. Soven
La Salle College, Philadelphia

Many of the teaching approaches employed in freshman composition courses do not pay sufficient attention to the three basic features of expository discourse: generalizing, specifying, and clarifying. I have developed a series of assignments and exercises designed to increase students' awareness of these characteristics and to teach them how to incorporate the characteristics into their writing. The assignments are based on assumptions that are compatible with modern learning theory and with recent research about the cognitive development of young adults:

1. Young adults are quite capable of analysis and synthesis of abstract as well as concrete information. They can think about ideas as well as about their firsthand experiences.

2. An awareness of students' thinking processes enables them to control those processes better.

3. Skills such as writing should be taught by providing opportunities for practice and for teacher response to those practice efforts.

4. A series of sequentially more complex tasks of conceptualization is effective in promoting the development of skills that are heavily dependent upon thinking.

The longer assignments are based on James Moffett's classification of discourse in terms of the writer's (or speaker's) "distance" from his subject. Moffett suggests that as the subject of a message becomes further removed in space and time from the sender, the sender of the message must analyze and synthesize more information in order to form meaningful generalizations. Moffett distinguishes discourse that describes:

1. what is happening (recording)
2. what happened (reporting)
3. what happens (generalizing)
4. what may happen (theorizing)

Moving from the "what is happening" category to the "what happens" category, the sender of the message must range over a greater field when generalizing about experience. The "what may happen" category involves the combining of generalizations to form a new, more comprehensive generalization.

Moffett gives the following example of this progression of abstraction. He contrasts a police log of events on a certain evening to the police station's annual summary and then to a theoretical essay on trends of crime in the United States. The author of the essay on crime is further removed in space and time from the concrete referents of that report than the police officer who wrote the evening log.[1]

The series of assignments I have designed (see Figure 1) are based loosely on Moffett's recording and generalizing categories. Early assignments require students to make generalizations about firsthand experiences. Students progress to developing generalizations about a number of similar experiences and then about experiences more different than they are alike. They move on to a set of assignments that requires them to synthesize increasingly more abstract written materials, starting with newspaper Op-Ed articles and progressing to formal essays. Finally, they are asked to do what Mina Shaughnessy calls "retrieving the history of an idea"[2] by working back from a generalization to the particulars that support it. The instructions for this last assignment require the student to convince the reader of the truth of a statement that the writer has thought about in the past.

The idea behind this set of assignments is that by having students first write about personal experiences and then progress to writing about ideas, they are obligated to understand how one proceeds to higher levels of abstraction. They are forced to understand the notion of a hierarchy of ideas ranging from the very concrete to the very abstract.

While a progression of assignments of this type serves to help students understand how to generalize and synthesize different types of information and increases their awareness of the degree of abstraction of their own statements, it does not necessarily encourage an analysis of the meaning of the generalizations themselves. Richard Ohmann argues persuasively that merely advising students to add detail or to be more specific can prevent them from coming to terms with what they mean and from exploring the complexity of their own ideas.[3] Language analysis, a series of techniques for clarifying the meaning of concepts, provides a mechanism whereby students can learn to define what they really mean before they amass evidence to support that meaning.[4] They learn to identify propositions hidden in the original generalization and to see the necessity for clarifying their intended meaning to their readers whenever multiple meanings are possible. For example, if they have said "Education is

1. The Report
   Purpose: to give the reader an impression of a particular place

   Visit some place of business or a particular location on campus or in
   the city. Observe your surroundings, talk with the people present, and
   then write an account of your visit. Use your narrative to convey your
   impression of the place, to catch the atmosphere of your surroundings.

2. The Profile
   Purpose: to give your reader an impression of what happens routinely
            in a particular place or situation

   Return several times to the same location. Carefully observe what
   happens and talk to the people present. Write a paper in which you
   tell what happens routinely in this place.

3. Profile of Readings
   Purpose: to tell your reader what several articles about the same
            subject have in common

   Read three articles appearing on the Op-Ed page of the newspaper that
   discuss a subject currently in the news. Develop a generalization
   about the subject based on the content of the three articles.

4. Thematic Collection of Incidents
   Purpose: to demonstrate to your reader similarities among seemingly
            different situations, incidents, places, or people

   Recall several incidents, places, people that seem to have something
   in common. Develop a generalization demonstrating the common features
   of the subject.

5. Thematic Collection of Readings
   Purpose: to demonstrate to your reader the similarities among three
            articles on different subjects

   Read three Op-Ed articles on different subjects. Develop a generalization expressing an idea common to all of these articles.

6. Thematic Collection of Essays
   Purpose: to demonstrate to your reader the similarities among three
            essays on different subjects

   Read three essays on different subjects. Develop a generalization
   expressing an idea common to all of these essays.

7. The Supported Generalization
   Purpose: to convince your reader of the truth of your generalizations
            about a given subject

   Make a general statement that seems true to you about a given subject
   that you have thought about or read about or that you are familiar
   with because of personal experience. Write a paper in which you
   support this generalization.

Figure 1. Abbreviated list of Moffett-based assignments.

1. Clarify the meaning of one of the following underlined words by developing two model cases to illustrate the word. List the features of meaning that might appear in a definition of the word.

   a. He was very <u>angry</u> with himself for what had happened.
   b. She is a very <u>congenial</u> hostess.
   c. Painters and authors are very <u>creative</u> people.

2. Clarify the meaning of one of the following underlined words by developing a model case and a contrary case. List the features of meaning that might appear in a definition of the word.

   a. <u>Punishment</u> is necessary in order to prevent <u>crime</u>.
   b. <u>Maturity</u> is a very important quality.
   c. It is important to achieve <u>independence</u> when you are a young adult.

3. Clarify the meaning of one of the following concepts by developing a model case, a contrary case, and a borderline case. List the features of meaning that might be included in a definition of the concept.

   a. <u>Education</u> is important in a technological society.
   b. In many countries people are denied <u>intellectual freedom</u>.
   c. The <u>women's liberation</u> movement has had a great impact on society.

4. Clarify the meaning of one of the following concepts by using at least two cases. Write a lexical or range definition of the concept.

   a. The "<u>energy crisis</u>" has been underestimated by public officials.
   b. The "<u>back-to-basics</u>" movement is going to be detrimental to our children's education.
   c. Our country prides itself on <u>equal opportunity</u> for all.

5. Write a definition in terms of observable qualities for two of the words or concepts you have previously clarified. Be sure to include all features of meaning in your definition.

6. Analyze the meaning of one of the concepts you have defined. What social values are threatened or served by this concept?

7. Choose a concept to clarify and analyze. Choose from the various language analysis techniques we have practiced to clarify and analyze your concept.

Figure 2. Sample language analysis assignments.

important in our society," they should feel obligated to clarify the meaning of "education" and "society" before defending or disagreeing with the proposition.

To focus attention on the language analysis aspects of writing within the confines of a one-semester composition course, I begin by introducing strategies for generating model cases, detailed examples of different meanings of a particular concept (see Figure 2). The following paragraph might be a model case involving "independence."

> John has left home. He plans to live alone from now on. He will earn his own money, take care of his domestic needs, and solve his own problems.

This model case suggests that independence implies taking care of oneself without help from others. Additional model cases will suggest other features of the meaning of "independence," which the students can then use to clarify their own intended meanings of the concept. A more detailed discussion of model cases as well as other language analysis techniques useful in teaching composition can be found in *Thinking with Concepts* by John Wilson, a textbook used in British secondary schools.[5]

I believe that this curriculum, based on combining language analysis exercises with a set of assignments requiring students to develop and support increasingly more abstract generalizations, is particularly useful for teaching composition. While all writing instruction requires students to develop, clarify, and elaborate generalizations, traditional writing curricula approach these principles of exposition only indirectly. The emphasis in *this* curriculum is to expose the process of developing, clarifying, and supporting a thesis statement. By practicing with a variety of information on different abstraction levels, the students gain insight into the process itself.

Notes

1. James Moffett and Betty Jane Wagner, *Student-Centered Language Arts, K-13,* 2nd ed. (Boston: Houghton Mifflin Co., 1976), p. 14.

2. Mina Shaughnessy, *Errors and Expectations* (New York: Oxford University Press, 1977), p. 241.

3. Richard Ohmann, "Use Definite, Specific, Concrete Language," *College English* 41 (1979): 390-98.

4. Instructors interested in language analysis may write to Margot K. Soven, La Salle College, Philadelphia, Pennsylvania, 19141.

5. John Wilson, *Thinking with Concepts* (Cambridge: Cambridge University Press, 1976).

Journal Writing—The Quiet Time

Barbara Leonard Warren
Casa Grande Union High School, Arizona

Ah, listen to the quietness! Ten wonderful minutes of silence. If you listen, you can hear the fluorescent lights humming, and the clock making its tiny jumps to the next minute.

No, it's not my planning period. It's not lunch time. It's not even those last few precious minutes before the first bell in the morning. Instead, it's the beginning of third period. The bell has just rung, and my twenty-seven ninth graders are busily writing in their journals. They came into the room as noisily as usual, but they quickly found their journals in the box and were ready to write when the bell rang. A miracle? No, just a ten-minute respite filled with writing and creativity.

When I started journal writing with my high school freshmen several years ago, I had only two rules—the entries must be legal and not obscene. Within a few weeks, however, I'd added another rule—entries had to be in English—because I'd found myself baffled by the shorthand and Spanish some students had used.

This year I've added another requirement. Each Monday, after my students have described the wonders of their weekends, I dictate a specific assignment that they must complete during that week. They star the entry so I can find it easily.

I read the journals every few weeks but do not make any comments in them. The grade is based on whether the students have actually written for the full ten minutes each day (two sentences are hardly adequate!) and whether they have completed the weekly assignments. Students are free to check their letter grades, recorded in my grade book, at any time.

Some students wish I would write responses in their journals, but I can't possibly manage that with over 100 entries a day. Whenever I find something disturbing, however, I speak privately with the student concerned.

A few years ago a girl wrote that her father had been beating her but stressed she was afraid to talk with anyone about it for fear he would hurt her even more. I finally convinced her to tell the guidance counselor, and he referred her to the proper authorities. Within twenty-four hours, the girl had been removed from her father's custody and sent to live with her mother in another state. I felt that if this were the only good that journal writing ever accomplished, it had been very successful indeed.

But I've found all sorts of other "goods" along the way. The ten minutes of concentrated writing at the beginning of the period serves a number of purposes. Journal writing gets the students into the classroom and settled down very quickly. Instead of stopping to tell their friends about their weekend dates, their problems with the mean teacher during second period, the test they just failed, they write everything down. News, fury, distress, happiness—everything is recorded and preserved for future reference. Even students who begrudge every second of writing tend to enjoy rereading their journals at the end of the year. They're amazed at all the great things they'd forgotten, and they spend lots of time sharing entries with their friends.

Journal writing also makes students more comfortable with the act of writing. They are no longer afraid of a blank piece of paper and find that they do indeed have something to say. I've used a number of the weekly assignments as the basis of composition writing, after noting that the students had responded to them in great detail. Thus instead of worrying about content, they can spend most of their time on grammar and mechanics. Their compositions have improved dramatically as a result.

I've discovered a number of sources of weekly assignments—magazines, newspapers, college professors, friends, psychology books, and even grammar texts. I keep each assignment on a separate piece of typing paper in a file folder, so I can add to them at any time and select whatever appeals to me most each Monday morning.

The first entry of the year was quite detailed: "Write a description of yourself and consider the fact that I have never seen you before. What do you look like? What kinds of things do you like to eat, to read, to watch on TV, to do in your spare time? What quality or qualities do you like best about yourself? What do you like least about yourself? Can you change that quality? Tell me anything else you would like me to know about you."

This entry took several days to complete, but the results were delightful. As a result, I was able to start matching names and faces almost immediately and I learned about my new students much more quickly and in much more detail than ever before.

Several other topics that have worked well so far include:

What three books would you want to have with you if you were stranded on a deserted island? The majority of students responded with the traditional texts on building shacks, identifying edible plants, and killing wild animals. One enterprising boy immediately opted for a book on how to get off a deserted island. A surprising number wanted teenage novels so they wouldn't feel so lonely. And several wanted puzzle and riddle books to keep them entertained. One girl wanted a long novel with parallel translations in English, Spanish, French, and German so she could make a dictionary, set up a grammar, and teach herself the other languages!

If you could be anyone in the world, who would you choose and why? I'd expected my ninth graders to choose movie or rock stars and was surprised (and secretly pleased) by the number who decided they would choose to be themselves. They were completely satisfied with their lives, they announced, and they certainly didn't need the escapism of being someone else.

What is the one thing you wish your parents would do? Have they ever done this before? What happened? I'd expected answers like, "I wish they'd let me stay out later on weekends" or "I wish they'd let me play the stereo louder." Although a few hoped their parents would find better jobs or move back to former communities where all their friends still lived, most wanted their parents to be able to take some time off and get away from the family for a week or so.

Describe your most embarrassing moment. As you think about it, do you still feel as embarrassed now as you did then? While a number of students had overcome their embarrassment about falling down stairs, dropping an armload of books, or being splashed by a car driving through a mud puddle, many still felt as upset as the day the embarrassing moment had occurred. As they were writing, their faces became flushed and their hands clenched their pens tightly. Even those moments that had occurred years before seemed absolutely real to the students, who were sure that everyone else also remembered every dreadful detail.

One day I gave an assignment that required the students to get out and do something before writing their reactions:

> For the next twenty-four hours, you are to smile and say hello to everyone you meet—particularly those people you meet in the corridors, near lockers, and on the stairs. As you smile and say hello, watch their reactions very carefully. Then tomorrow, describe in your journal the various reactions you noticed. How did the majority of people react? Did they smile and respond? Did they laugh? Did they speak at all? What were the strangest reactions you received? What did you learn from this experiment?

Although a few students received very negative reactions, the majority found that people would either stare in amazement or inadvertently smile back and say hello. Some were openly ridiculed, but others generated lots of comments. A week after the assignment, one girl confided in her journal that she had become great friends with a boy she had smiled and said hello to for the first time in the corridor.

As the year rushes to a close, I'm looking forward to reading the last entry before returning the completed journals: "You've kept a journal for nine months now. Please reread it and consider what you have learned during the course of this year. What kinds of changes have occurred in your life? Were these changes good or bad? How else could you have reacted to some of the situations you've described? What is your reaction to having reread the entire journal?"

And as my students are rereading and writing, I will be doing the same because I also have employed those precious ten minutes at the beginning of each period to write in my own journal. By the end of the school year, I too will have filled a whole journal, and I look forward to taking the time to evaluate my own year. I also look forward to starting my summer journal, which I intend to fill with vacation adventures and journal-writing ideas for next year's ninth graders.

4 Structuring the Evaluation of Writing

Facilitating the Peer Critiquing of Writing

Janice Hays
University of Colorado, Colorado Springs

In recent years, many writing instructors have adopted the practice of having students read and critique each others' papers. The benefits of this kind of activity are many: reading their classmates' papers offers students peer models to which they can relate more immediately than they can to the professional readings that we so frequently urge upon them and critiquing other students' papers helps them to develop their own critical skills. Perhaps the most important benefit is that writing for their peers gives students a live audience for their work and thus strengthens their sense of the rhetorical situation in their writing. A specific audience enables students to become aware of readers' needs for context, clarity, and sufficient information in a piece of writing. In turn, such awareness helps students to assume the reader's perspective as they compose.

Careful structuring is the key to successful peer evaluation of writing, and as instructors who have tried peer critiquing well know, it does not just come about automatically. The logistics of making papers available to the class must be carefully engineered so that the process runs smoothly, and the critiquing procedures have to be carefully worked out and certain pitfalls avoided. If each of these matters is attended to, peer critiquing can be the heart of the writing classroom and, indeed, the most educative part of it.

I would like to suggest some strategies and structures that I and many of my colleagues have found to be effective in implementing peer critiquing in our writing courses. While the procedures described apply primarily to the college writing class, many of these techniques work equally well with high school and junior high school students and, after some modification, with even younger writers.

At the beginning of a term, I explain to my writing students that they will be publishing their papers for their peers. I also tell them that if at any point they write something they do not want to share with the group or with the class, they are welcome simply to tell me of their wish for privacy and I will respect it. In six years of using peer critiquing on a weekly basis in my writing classes, I have had this happen only three times. Students usually look forward to writing for their peers and sharing their writing with them.

The critiquing setting can be handled in several ways. Students can choose partners with whom they exchange papers, or they can form small groups in which to critique their work so that each writer gets the benefit of feedback from several readers. With younger students the partner arrangement might be preferable. Partners or groups can be either temporary, changing from week to week, or permanent, extending over much of the semester. It is advisable to let students choose their partners or the members of their groups. If they have selected the peers with whom they want to associate, they take more responsibility for making the critiquing process work than they do if a teacher has imposed these arrangements upon them.

In the early weeks of the semester, I explain to students that they will be placed in different groups for each of three weeks, so that they can get to know each other and have some experience working with all members of the class. After that time, students choose the groupings that they want for the rest of the semester; I ask students to tell me the four people with whom they would like to form a group and to give me first, second, and third choices so that I have some flexibility in case everyone in the class chooses to be in a group with the same two people. Students hand in their written preferences, and I then make up the groups. If students are unhappy with a group assignment, I will try to make changes. At two or three points during the semester, I also give groups the opportunity to shift membership, but group members rapidly form bonds and seem to prefer to stay together for an entire term. Groups appoint a facilitator to take charge of critiquing sessions, either permanently or on a rotating basis. If groups are going to engage in other collaborative learning activities besides critiquing, a recorder is appointed to make written records of the group's business.

In setting up peer critiquing, one must next arrange for the duplication and distribution of papers. If students are working with only a partner, they simply exchange their papers with one another during the class session prior to the critiquing day. Of course, it is also possible for students not to exchange papers in advance but to take turns on the critiquing day reading their papers to each other, with the listener then giving the writer feedback. This arrangement can be used either with partners or in groups. While the technique is useful for building listening skills, it takes up a great deal of classroom time—often a problem in college classes that meet only two or three times weekly. Further, students cannot do detailed critiquing assignments unless they have the paper to study before the critiquing session.

The first step in setting up a system of advance publication and distribution is to require students to type or write their papers on ditto masters. A generously budgeted institution can provide students with the masters; those on stricter rations can require students to buy their own. However, if it is not feasible to print all papers that students write, the following system works nearly as well pedagogically as duplicating all the papers for all the assignments: each week two students in each critiquing group are appointed "writers-of-the-week," and one student is designated "all-class-writer-of-the-week." These names are distributed to the class at the same time as the weekly assignments, a full week in advance of the date on which papers are due. Thus, only writers-of-the-week must write their papers on ditto masters.

The ditto masters must be turned in by an established time on the day when writing assignments are due. If students miss this deadline, it is their responsibility to bring to class enough duplicated copies of their papers to distribute to the critiquing group, with two copies to the instructor. (Some students prefer to pay for photocopying rather than struggle with typing on ditto masters.) About ten copies each of the group writers' papers and enough copies of the all-class writer's paper to distribute to the full class are run off. This amount of dittoing, assembling, and stapling is manageable on a weekly basis. In settings in which all the students' papers are being published, the instructor can have the group facilitator distribute copies—or arrange some sort of advance pickup system outside the teacher's office (a cardboard box with indexed dividers works fine).

In the early weeks of the semester, there are, inevitably, problems with these arrangements. Predictably some students will type or write their papers on the wrong surface of the ditto master. Other students will not get their dittos in on time, some will be confused about whether or not they are to put their papers on dittos, and so on. However, after about three weeks everybody gets the hang of things, and the process runs like clockwork. It is important *not* to deviate from the established procedures. A student who shows up an hour after the dittoing deadline, ditto master in hand, simply has to make photocopies or else use a ditto machine in some other department. After one such experience, the student usually gets the ditto master in on time.

Further, in every writing class there will be a few students who occasionally don't get their papers in when they are writers-of-the-week (the closer the class to the developmental level, the more apt this is to be the case). It is important, I think, not to embarrass students for these lapses, but their failures should not be allowed to ruin the critiquing session. Thus a certain amount of contingency planning and last-minute flexibility is necessary: if a group writer has failed to turn in a ditto master or duplicated papers, students critique the all-class writer's paper as part of their group work. If an all-class writer fails to turn in a paper, a group writer's paper is substituted and enough copies are duplicated for the entire class.

At the heart of the successful use of peer critiquing is the structuring of the critiquing sessions. They must be carefully set up to prevent their becoming a pooling of vague generalities and ignorances, their deteriorating into rap sessions, or, most destructive of all, their becoming negative experiences for the writers being evaluated. Firm ground rules must be made, and there are several approaches to doing this. Instructors who like to have students read their papers aloud to each other should require listeners to do two things only: state what they liked best about the paper and indicate any places that could use further information. This feedback alone is delivered to the writer.

I prefer to use a more detailed critiquing structure that asks students to look for specific rhetorical and stylistic points in the papers they are evaluating. However, the following rules are established right from the beginning, and during the early weeks of the class I circulate from group to group to be sure that these rules are being adhered to:

1. Students should always begin their evaluations with positive feedback, telling the writer what they particularly liked about the paper. They should be specific.

2. Students are never to make negative remarks about each others' papers. They may report upon those places where they needed more information or became confused, and they may make suggestions that will help the writer to improve the paper. (Specific details about how to structure this kind of critiquing assignment are given later.)

3. Students are not to critique each others' grammar or syntax. This rule is necessary for two reasons: first, students are so conditioned to regard writing evaluation as error hunting that left to their own devices, they will focus upon nothing else; second, they know very little about grammar and will identify all sorts of things as grammatical errors that aren't, while missing errors that are present. What they should look for in the papers that they are evaluating is the presence or absence of certain syntactical devices that we have studied—but only after they have evaluated larger structures in the discourse.

Actually, I have found that most students are very supportive in dealing with one another's writing (they also know that if they are disparaging in discussing a writer's work, they are apt to get the same treatment when they are writers-of-the-week). The very occasional student who is making negative evaluations is simply told not to do so.

Students are given the week's critiquing assignment one class period prior to the time established for the critiquing sessions. For instance, the week's papers and critiquing assignment are distributed on Monday for a critiquing session on Wednesday. Students prepare their critiques outside of class, making notes right on their copy of the writer's paper.

On Wednesday, at the beginning of the class, I critique the all-class writer's paper. Doing so enables me to discuss the rhetorical and syntactical points that we have worked on in the unit's writing assignment and, equally important, to model for students what a paper critique should be. (I also tape critiques of individual papers for students, which serves as another kind of modeling.) Students then spend thirty to forty-five minutes in their small groups. One writer at a time is critiqued; each student in the group has three to five minutes of time to give that writer feedback. Finally, the writer has five minutes for response before the group turns its attention to the other writer-of-the-week. At the end of the class hour, students hand their written critiques in to be graded. At the beginning of the term, students are ineffectual and overly general in their evaluations; by midsemester, they are giving each other detailed, specific, perceptive, and helpful evaluations.

In developing a specific critiquing assignment, I ask students first to give the writer positive feedback; then I have them look at several points involving the paper's larger structure and one or two dealing with syntactical matters. The following steps outline a critiquing assignment that I use midway through a basic writing course. Students, who have written about a significant experience that they have had, critique the papers of the writers-of-the-week by performing the following procedures.

1. Find one portion of the paper that you really like and tell the writer about it. Be specific.

2. Mark any places that you did not understand and be prepared to tell the writer what your problem was. Explain your problem with the passage to the writer.

3. Find three places where the writer either has done a good job of developing a point or needs to do a better job of developing it using examples, illustrations, details, and so on. Be specific: for example, "Just saying that the old man had a seizure doesn't help me really see him," or "Your use of the detail about the old man's

gasping for breath and turning blue makes me vividly aware of how frightening the man's seizure must have been."

4. What do you think the experience meant to the writer? Has the writer made that meaning clear?

5. Find three places where the writer either has done a good job of clarifying the relationships among ideas through the use of joining devices or needs to use joining devices to make these relationships clear. Mark these places "JOIN +" or "JOIN −," depending upon whether the writer has made effective use of such devices.

6. Pick one place that you have marked "JOIN +" and explain why the joining or relating device is effective. For example, "When John says, 'Because I worked all summer instead of going to the beach every day, I was able to buy a car,' the *because* shows the reason why he was able to buy the car: he worked all summer."

7. Pick one place that you have marked "JOIN −" and suggest to the writer a way that the ideas could be joined or related effectively. For example, "Instead of writing, 'I disliked the job. I worked at it all summer,' try, 'I disliked the job; *however*, I worked at it all summer.'"

At this point in the semester, the class has studied both subordination and coordination (the "joining" devices referred to in the assignment). This assignment gives them a model for informing a writer about how to develop a point and how to join or relate two ideas more effectively. This kind of modeling is necessary to instruct students in how to give each other text-related feedback—as opposed to generalities such as, "I really liked the paper"—and that the degree of prescriptiveness that the assignment imposes is necessary with beginning writers. Simply telling students to look for effective or ineffective examples of joining, for instance, yields nothing. Giving them a specific and manageable number of such devices to look for, three, with the additional requirement that they improve upon one of those three, does work.

As students reach the end of the basic writing or entry-level freshman composition course, or if they are more advanced writers, they can use a descriptive outline similar to one that Kenneth Bruffee discusses in *A Short Course in Writing*[1] and that Richard Beach uses for self-assessment of papers at the University of Minnesota.[2] This form asks students to state the paper's main point, to summarize each paragraph in one sentence, to state in one sentence what each paragraph accomplishes (for example, "This paragraph introduces the paper's main idea and develops it with an explanation"), and to note any places at which they were confused or wanted more information. It is essential to model this kind of form for students; otherwise, they will simply summarize each paragraph twice rather than summarizing and then identifying the paragraph's function in the paper as a whole. After working with these forms for a while, however, students develop a strong sense of how papers work— and they develop a sense of writers as people who adopt strategies and make choices as they write.

A carefully prepared and structured peer-critiquing session can be the most valuable learning experience of the entire writing course. Such sessions heighten students' awareness that they are communicating to readers when they write, and the sessions vastly increase students' motivation both to write and to read each others' writing.

Notes

1. Kenneth Bruffee, *A Short Course in Writing*, 2nd ed. (Cambridge, Mass: Winthrop, 1980).

2. Reported upon at the 1981 CCCC Convention in Dallas, Texas.

Structuring the Classroom for Peer Revision of Composition

Leila Christenbury
James Madison University, Harrisonburg, Virginia

Many English teachers have turned to peer revision in their classrooms to improve student compositions. The practice of having students look at other students' work and offer advice, suggestions, and comments has many positive benefits: students not only receive a variety of opinions on their written work, but their own revision skills are sharpened through the practice of looking at others' efforts. Finally, many teachers have found that student suggestions for revision of composition are often as beneficial and perceptive as wholly instructor-dominated suggestions for revision.

Despite the above benefits, however, some teachers are understandably hesitant to embark upon student revision in their classrooms. Many are unsure of how to structure peer revision so that it is not only useful but also orderly. The following are suggestions for structuring the classroom for peer revision including warm-up activities, grouping, the establishment of roles and tasks, and reinforcement.

Warm-Up Activities

While many students are familiar with group work, they may be unsure of how to operate in a group that is to consider a piece of written work and offer suggestions for improvements. One method to introduce a class to peer revision is the so-called fishbowl technique. The strong point of this technique is that students watch a type of "living play" and can witness the dynamics of a revision group in action. In addition, all students in the class participate in this activity.

Place three to five desks in the center of a circle of desks. Have three to five students sit in the center and discuss a composition that the class has read. The rest of the class is to listen to the discussion and take notes on the model group's interaction and comments. After about five minutes of discussion, stop the model group and let the class assess what they have witnessed. Then, change the model group so that a different group of students continues the discussion of the paper. Repeat the process a third time if necessary. Do not be tempted to vary the paper; keep the composition in question the same for all groups.

By the third and possibly even the second discussion, the focus will move from the composition itself—with which the class is becoming increasingly familiar—to the group process of revision. Students will thus be able to witness not just the composition assessment but also peer interaction in a revision group.

Another technique using group work is to have students, in groups, read their compositions aloud and have the group find something they specifically like about each composition. This activity is called "Smile Time." Students practice on two or three assignments until they are comfortable with their roles. An atmosphere of trust is soon established and students, after the experience of "Smile Time," are more comfortable with each other and more willing to suggest substantial alterations in others' compositions.

Grouping

Pairs of students can work effectively in peer revision, although changing pairs is often necessary as students can become stale in their suggestions and interactions after a few sessions with one another. Studies suggest groups of three to five are also effective, but these groups also should be changed after two or three sessions to avoid boredom and staleness. It is also possible, after some time in one group, to have students choose two or more people with whom they have never worked in order to enrich variety and to expose students to others' writing styles and interests.

The placement of students within groups can be made randomly. If a class is somewhat homogeneous, it is possible for students to work with friends or desk neighbors and achieve positive results. Composition samples, however, are a good idea when the students are new to the teacher and when a more "scientific" grouping is desired. A teacher can read composition samples and generally rank students on a three-point scale. Depending upon the size of the revision groups, the teacher can then create a heterogeneous arrangement of students who respectively receive a ranking of 1, 2, and 3 (for a group of three), a ranking of 1, 2, 2, and 3 (for a group of four), or even an arrangement of 1, 1, 2, 3, and 3 (for a group of five). From personal experience, a mixture of male and female is a desirable goal, as is a mixture of races. In general, this heterogeneous grouping of students will insure that students of varying abilities can interact, providing exposure to different levels of writing.

Another method of grouping students, either after an initial sample has been obtained and a group established or for an initial grouping, is to use composition grades on specific assignments. It is wise to remember, however, that student grades will naturally fluctuate on specific assignments; for example, a student who enjoys description but not argumentation may receive a higher grade on one assignment than on the other. Thus, it is possible that the use of a more general composition sample will more accurately determine a student's writing level. At any rate, the teacher must be sensitive to the dangers of pigeonholing a student through the results of one composition assignment.

Establishment of Roles and Tasks

Much confusion and frustration can result from peer revision if the students are not sure of their tasks or roles in their specific groups. It is possible to assign students specific roles, such as in Audrey J. Roth's author/editor/proofreader schema where students, in groups of threes, are alternately the author of a piece, the editor of a second piece, and the proofreader of a third piece.[1] While such role distinctions are, to a certain extent, artificial—editors will notice and comment upon items assigned to a proofreader, and proofreaders may see and comment upon questions that might be left to an editor—the use of author/editor/proofreader roles is effective in that it provides the student with a specific task to perform within a specific time period. For a sample assignment sheet for students, see Figure 1.

Another way to clarify student tasks for revision is to give them a worksheet tailored to the specific assignment (see Figure 2). Using these worksheets students must extract from the composition specific sentences, words, or lists of characteristics. The use of worksheets not only defines the task for the student revisor but also gives the teacher an index of the student's effort in his or her revision group.

Reinforcement

The teacher who uses peer revision groups or pairs should remain in the classroom to offer help and to answer questions; however, the teacher should avoid becoming overly involved in any group. Students, as all of us know, suspect that the teacher has the magic answers, and if a teacher consistently enters into a group's deliberations, it is quite possible that the group's authority will be permanently eroded. Nevertheless, a circulating teacher is reassuring to students and can provide invaluable help with questions that a student revisor is unable to answer.

There are three members of the group, each of whom alternately takes the role of author, editor, and then proofreader. Each member, in turn:

presents his or her written work
edits a group member's work
proofreads a member's work

Note: The teacher will call time for each step and indicate when the editor should hand his or her composition to the proofreader.

As an author, your responsibility is to present a clean, readable rough draft. For the purposes of this plan, please double-space your draft.

As an editor, your responsibility is to review a rough draft and ask yourself--and the author--the following:

What is the main idea of the piece?

What aspects of the main idea are evident?

Are sufficient examples, support, or illustrations used?

Are there smooth transitions between ideas? between paragraphs?

Is the end of the paper satisfactory?

Does the reader of this piece have any lingering questions or doubts?

As a proofreader, your responsibility is to review an edited rough draft and ask yourself--and the author--the following:

Is the language concrete, specific?

Are words used accurately?

Is there any repetition of words or ideas?

Is there correct spelling? punctuation? subject/verb agreement? pronoun/antecedent agreement?

INSTRUCTIONS: Count off one, two, and three. Then:

Author One hands work to Editor Two who hands work to Proofreader Three.

Author Two hands work to Editor Three who hands work to Proofreader One.

Author Three hands work to Editor One who hands work to Proofreader Two.

Figure 1. Sample assignment sheet for editorial groups of three (author, editor, proofreader).

Author

Editor/Proofer

Date

1. Thesis statement

2. Concluding statement

3. Things/Persons/Places being compared or contrasted

4. Examples or details that support thesis statement (list only) and
   compare or contrast

5. Strongest sentence

6. Weakest sentence

7. Words that may be misspelled
   a.   b.   c.
   d.   e.   f.

8. Words that may be misused
   a.   b.   c.
   d.   e.   f.

9. Verbal indicators ("similarly," "in contrast to," etc.)

10. Informal outline

Figure 2. Sample worksheet/checklist designed for a comparison/contrast essay.

Another simple way to reinforce the group work is to ask the students to attach to their final drafts the rough drafts with student comments and suggestions or the worksheets with the same comments. In this manner, the teacher is giving emphasis to the student revision suggestions and is also in a position to assess whether a specific student or group is actually on task. Finally, it is also possible to consult with both the author of the essay and the revisor regarding a final draft. While such a conference should not be a punitive one—a student revisor may honestly misinterpret another student's writing or may legitimately miss a spelling error or transitional problem—placing emphasis upon the student revisor will tend to reinforce the importance of that student's role in the production of a good and clear piece of writing.

Lastly, after a revision group has completed its work and each member has a final draft ready to submit for a grade, it is possible to ask the group to choose only one composition to be graded with the understanding that the grade for that composition will be the grade for each individual in the group. A few cautions are in order: the group should carefully discuss the possible options and should submit with the chosen essay a point-by-point rationale expressing why they feel this essay is a good one (or the best one). Also, each member of the group must have the opportunity to participate in the revision of each essay. Of course, giving each member of the group the grade of the submitted essay is optional; the teacher may find the practice of choosing and revising one essay is sufficient. Nevertheless, a group effort on a single composition and grade may reinforce the importance of the group's revision task.

Teachers whose experiences with peer revision were unsatisfactory might consider these structuring devices. While most students are willing to share their writing (unless it is of a highly personal nature), they need, first, an indication of how a group might work, provided through the warm-up activities; second, a logical student arrangement, provided through grouping; third, a specific list of criteria, provided through the establishment of roles and tasks; and, finally, positive feedback for their efforts, provided through reinforcement. If students are given these four structuring tools, they will benefit from receiving many opinions on their own work and, in turn, will become more sensitive to writing through their efforts as revisors and editors. Through careful structuring, peer revision of student composition can be an effective teaching—and learning—tool for our student writers.

Note

1. Audrey J. Roth, "Editorial Groups," in *Classroom Practices and the Teaching of English, 1979-80: How to Handle the Paper Load*, ed. Gene Stanford (Urbana, Ill.: NCTE, 1980) pp. 67-71.

Ranking Writing

Beverly Lyon Clark
Wheaton College, Norton, Massachusetts

While leading faculty seminars on writing, I realized that to focus our discussions of evaluative criteria we needed to examine student writing. And I discovered that the best discussions derived from a ranking exercise: four paragraphs written by college students were handed out, and participants were asked to rank the paragraphs, using whatever criteria they thought appropriate. The participants conferred in groups of five to see if they could reach a consensus, then the larger group reconvened to discuss the rankings—and the criteria. For in trying to reach a consensus it is necessary to share criteria, to discuss what is wrong or right with a paragraph. The ultimate goal of this ranking exercise was to discuss criteria and to make everyone aware of their own personal preferences and how they may differ from another's (and not to convert everyone to the same standard, or at least not entirely). Asking people to rank paragraphs and reach a consensus gives an urgency to the discussion that it otherwise lacks. Ranking the paragraphs requires making a personal commitment, which loosens tongues and sharpens analysis.

This ranking exercise proved so energizing that I now use it in a number of settings: in teaching writing to freshmen, who need to diagnose difficulties and to learn how to improve their own paragraphs, and in training peer writing tutors, who need to diagnose difficulties and then to try out tutoring techniques. I've also used ranking exercises in discussions of literature, asking students to rank Meg, Jo, Beth, and Amy in order of preference or asking students to rank characters in *Pride and Prejudice* on a scale from emotion/nature to reason/civilization.

But I will concentrate here on the ranking of sample paragraphs. I use the following student paragraphs, each on the topic of energy and each supposed to incorporate some reference to solar power, clean fuels, cost, environment, and independence from foreign energy sources. The paragraphs reproduce the students' mistakes; two of them were written by the same student.

1. As the American economy continues its downward trend, econ-omists continue to emphasize the urgent need of an energy program. Some economists have investigated solar energy and feel it is the best choice. They contend that it will be inexpensive once instituted, and that it will not harm the environment. Furthermore they state that such an energy program will illimi-nate the United States fatal dependence on OPEC. In short, they state that the United States dependence on foriegn sourses has driven the economy into a recession and that such a program will reinvigorate the economy.

2. The use of fuel was never a problem for our grandparents but now the problem of fuel has become our concern. One problem is to find a way to produce solar power at a prices people can pay. But in order to do that we must become less dependent on foreign sources for our fuel. This would give the fuel producers an incentive to produce more fuel. The increase in production would bring down prices. When we become less dependent on them the production of fuel in our own country will increase. The key to energy is the increase of production in the U.S. and then the prices may go down.

3. We are aware of the high cost of oil from foreign countries for energy in this country. If we were to develop more and more solar power, we would have a much better environment. Granted, the initial cost of such a system would be high. We would also be a nation independent from foreign sources to meet the needs of energy.

   In the long run the system would be cheaper and give us the benefits of clean fuels and independence from foreign sources.

4. There is a great need to develop more solar power to help alleviate the energy crisis. Granted, there are some disavantages and one of them is the high initial cost of installing such a system. However, we would have a much better environment because we would have cleaner air. We would, also, be a nation independent from foreign sources to meet the needs of energy. In the long run the system would be cheaper and give us the benefits of clean fuels and independence from foreign sources.

Both students and faculty members generally reach agreement on the worst two and the best two: they generally rank number 1 and number 4 ahead of number 2 and number 3. (Number 3 and number 4 are "before" and "after" paragraphs.) But there is no immutable order: people need to understand why they rank the paragraphs as they do—what their prior-ities are—and they should become aware of how their particular priorities differ from others'.

Those who prefer number 1 to number 4 tend to favor stylistic flow and scholarly context (and tend not to be put off by spelling). Those who prefer number 4 favor directness. And those who prefer number 2 to number 3 tend to prefer a smooth flow from sentence to sentence, whatever the underlying logic: the writer knows how to use sentence connectives—for example, the third sentence begins with "But" and includes a demonstrative pronoun referring back to the preceding sentence—but what does "this" refer to, and does the writer really want to say that becoming less dependent on foreign sources will enable us to produce solar power that we can afford? Those who prefer number 3, on the other hand, can manage to ignore the focus implied in the first sentence.

Since number 3 and number 4 are "before" and "after" paragraphs, the exercise can also lead into a discussion of strategies for tutoring and teaching. The author of number 3 may know how to organize a paragraph but may have forgotten here—the writer may have discovered what to say while writing, may have done some exploratory free writing and then forgotten to rework it. In that case all that is necessary is a nudge— perhaps simply asking the author how the paragraph could be revised to make it easier for a reader to follow. In fact, however, the writer seemed still at sea when asked probing questions, and the teacher became more programmatic, suggesting that the writer start with a thesis statement, discuss disadvantages and advantages, and conclude with a more general statement.

The exercise can lead in other directions as well—such as practice for students in revising paragraphs. But, in any case, the initial ranking provides a concrete focus for discussion of writing and practice in evaluation. And the discussion is likely to be an energetic give-and-take among participants, with the discussion leader worried not about prodding the discussion into life but rather about how to cut it off.

5 Structuring Language Study

Easing the Burden of Teaching Vocabulary

Philip Holmes
Harvard School, North Hollywood, California

Katherine Moore
Harvard School, North Hollywood, California

As English teachers, we are more concerned than the teachers of any other subject with the students' development of that distinctive human endowment—language; hence, we must also be concerned with vocabulary study, for learning to speak, read, and write ever more intelligently requires, in part, making ever more discriminating judgments in diction. No doubt students would become more adept in their choice of vocabulary if every day in every class they were called upon to examine carefully a few words arising from the subject at hand. As it is, the burden of vocabulary development falls mainly on the English teacher, all the more so when the verbal test scores of the class are below the expectations of the community. The question, then, is how can we keep the students motivated the whole year so that they are steadily pushed beyond their current level of word knowledge and how can we do all this without sacrificing the time needed for important lessons in other areas. How is the English teacher to individualize the instruction, should students prove to have widely disparate verbal aptitudes? Last year, for instance, we gave all our tenth graders a test that roughly determined their working vocabulary. The results ranged from 7,000 to over 50,000 words.

The teacher's burden is little eased by the attention that vocabulary receives in most texts of grammar, literature, or composition in which vocabulary study is at best a unit, but often no more than a footnote. On the other hand, texts devoted entirely to vocabulary study may support a regular but detached routine that distracts students from the primary purposes of increasing their stock of words and refining their judgment of words and is considered by them to be "busy work." What is needed, then, is an approach to vocabulary study in which regular attention to words and their meanings is subordinated to the larger purposes of the

English program. The French schools at the turn of the century practiced such an approach, and in the 1912 volume of *Instructions*, issued by the French Minister of Education to secondary school teachers, the text states:

> The pupil must learn words, though never apart from things (i.e. from "what he sees" and "what he reads"); he must be able to seize their signification and the exact shade of their meaning; and he must become accustomed to finding the words quickly when he stands in need. Hence the value of exercises devoted especially to the study of vocabulary.[1]

The phrase "devoted especially to the study of vocabulary" makes clear that a student's lexical sophistication should not depend on a hope that a high number of the words encountered daily in discussion and in reading will be unconsciously assimilated. Rather, the student must attend consciously to words, not words "apart from things," but words in the context of "what he sees . . . and what he reads." And the outcome of this attention must be the "enlarging, sharpening, and quickening"[2] of the student's knowledge of words.

For many years we struggled without success to accomplish these ends through units on roots, through vocabulary-building books, and through lists of words from the readings. Then, two years ago we developed a new approach. This approach promotes more accurate reading; improves the student's command of idiom and grammar; adapts to individual differences, pressing each student to examine individual stocks of words; and requires very little of the teacher's effort to sustain.

The vocabulary program that we have found so productive and easy to sustain quickly establishes this general routine. At least twice a week the teacher, having introduced the students to the literature they are to read as homework, blocks out in that assignment one short passage whose entire vocabulary students are expected to know for the following day. The students record in a vocabulary notebook any and all words from the passage for which they could not easily and confidently think of a substitute as they read. Each word is to be recorded in a significant portion of the sentence from which it is drawn, and for each entry the student is to record, after consulting a dictionary, a semantically and grammatically equivalent expression. At the next meeting, the class will be tested twice on the exact significance of the passage. The work the students bring to the next meeting can be seen in the following samples from the notebook of a tenth grader. The entries in the first excerpt are based on a passage from a Jack London short story, "Love of Life," which was read early in the school year. Here the student found both words and metaphors difficult. His entries require many corrections, particularly in syntax (item 33) and also in spelling (item 37).

23. composed | *"composed* himself with *infinite precaution"*
calmed
24. infinite | never ending
25. precaution | safeguard
26. steeled | "he *steeled* himself to keep"
stiffened his mental state
27. suffocating | "above the *suffocating languor* that *lapped"*
28. languor |
29. lapped | move on little waves
30. wells | "through all the *wells* of his being"
space having the shape of a well
31. drowned | *"drowned* his *consciousness* bit by bit"
to drive out
32. consciousness | a state of being characterized by emotions, sensation, and thought
33. swimming | *"swimming* through *oblivion,* with a *faltering* stroke"
to move with a motion like that of swimming, glide
34. oblivion | forgetfulness
35. faltering | wavering
36. alchemy | "by some strange *alchemy* of soul"
process transforming something common to something precious
37. shed | "find another *shed* of will"
?

The entries in the second excerpt are based on Part Seven of *The Rime of the Ancient Mariner.* Here the student, anticipating corrections that might be made in class, has put question marks next to entries of which he is uncertain.

1. hermit | "this *hermit* good lives"
recluse
? 2. rears | "voice he *rears"*
bring up
? 3. plump | "hath a cushion *plump"*
group
4. skiff | "the *skiff*-boat neared"
a light rowboat

? 5. trow	"I *trow*"
	believe or think
? 6. fair	"those lights so many and *fair*"
	clear
7. sere	"they are and *sere*"
	withered
? 8. aught	"I never saw *aught*"
	anything
9. perchance	"unless *perchance* it were"
	perhaps
10. lag	"leaves that *lag*"
	fall behind
11. tod	"ivy-*tod* is heavy"
	bushy clump
12. owlet	"*owlet* whoops"
	young owl
13. fiendish	"hath a *fiendish* look"
	diabolical
?14. straight	"*straight* a sound was heard"

The practice of keeping a vocabulary notebook as a record of those words and expressions that the individual student encounters while reading and cannot readily comprehend reveals the relationship of vocabulary study to developing composition skills. Through keeping this notebook, which need never be collected or graded, the student repeatedly practices choosing the best word or phrase to express varied and often complex ideas. The student acquires the habit of "letting the meaning choose the word," as recommended by George Orwell in "Politics and the English Language." Furthermore, when the difficulty of comprehension lies in metaphor or phrasing, the student must often recast a portion of a sentence or produce a syntactically parallel phrase for a single word. Among our tenth graders, the average number of entries for a semester's work is 300, though students have entered as many as 1000 words. Fewer than 10 of 140 students entered 150 or fewer words.

That this notebook need never be collected is explained by the specifics of "test day." The teacher begins the lesson by briefly summarizing the day's reading or asking a student to do so. The short passage is then read aloud, and afterwards students are directed to review the vocabulary in their notebooks. Then the students put aside their texts and notebooks and write down from memory the expressions they judge to be synonymous with the several words and phrases that the teacher selects from the passage and dictates in context. The students turn in their tests; motivated by a desire to find out how well they did on the test, they reopen their texts and notebooks and prepare themselves for an oral examination of the significance of the whole passage.

The second part of the lesson begins with the teacher choosing one student as the principal for the day's five- to ten-minute recitation. Any student who has made an honest attempt to do the homework well should be able to complete a turn as the principal, although some pupils may need more help from their peers than others. Every principal who makes it to the end of the session is rewarded in the grade book. Any students who are called upon to help out with answers and make a good effort to do so are also rewarded. This practice not only encourages students to give attention to the lesson but also gives the teacher yet another exercise that motivates students to develop their linguistic abilities, without creating more after-hours paperwork. By the end of the year, all students should have had about the same number of chances at being both a principal and a supporting participant. At the start of the year, however, the more diligent and able students should be chosen for the "hot seat" since their performances help set the standards that the teacher wants to uphold.

Once picked, the principal-of-the-day slowly reads the passage aloud, enunciating each word clearly, pronouncing each word correctly, and giving each sentence the emphasis rightly required by the syntax and punctuation. Any time the principal fails in one of these three areas, the teacher should stop the reader and correct the error. The principal can also expect to be stopped and be questioned about the meaning of any word or phrase, be it literal or figurative. When the last sentence has been examined, the student must then reflect briefly on what significance the passage has in relation to the whole work.

During the course of this mental workout, the other students are on the alert for questions that might suddenly arise. They are also critically eying their notebooks, ready to correct any mistakes or to add any words and phrases whose meaning is unclear. Students are also to watch for those words whose semantic structure and family relationships are analyzed by the teacher. Students are expected to record the results of the analysis, and in this low-key way we incorporate the study of Greek and Latin roots into our program.

The incentive for all this correcting and adding is that at the end of each unit the students will take an exam on all the vocabulary that has come up for discussion. These unit tests have ten entries, among which are some metaphorical expressions, quoted in context, that the students must paraphrase. Usually the students take no more than ten minutes to complete a test; they exchange papers and, under teacher guidance, correct one another's work. Thus, with the exception of grading the short quizzes that precede oral recitations, the instructor has no paper marking to do. Nevertheless, several marks are recorded in the grade books to reflect each student's effort at improving his or her vocabulary. And except for unit tests, there are no tests to type and duplicate. In other words, the workload is put where it should be—on the students and not on the teacher. Our task is to select significant passages that are appropriately challenging to our students and to keep the discussions moving at a fast pace.

Here are two of the passages that have proven particularly effective in these discussions and a sample of the sort of questions asked of the principal. (Note that these are the passages on which the sample student notebook entries are based.)

"Love of Life" Jack London

He closed his eyes and composed himself with infinite precaution. He steeled himself to keep above the suffocating languor that lapped like a rising tide through all the wells of his being. It was very like a sea, this deadly languor that rose and rose and drowned his consciousness bit by bit. Sometimes he was all but submerged, swimming through oblivion with a faltering stroke; and again, by some strange alchemy of soul, he would find another shred of will and strike out more strongly.

The Rime of the Ancient Mariner, Part the Seventh

The skiff-boat neared: I heard them talk,
"Why, this is strange, I trow!
Where are those lights so many and fair,
That signal made but now?"

"Strange, by my faith!" the Hermit said—
"And they answered not our cheer!
The planks look warped! and see those sails,
How thin they are and sere!
I never saw aught like to them,
Unless perchance it were

"Brown skeletons of leaves that lag
My forest-brook along;
When the ivy-tod is heavy with snow,
And the owlet whoops to the wolf below,
That eats the she-wolf's young."

"Dear Lord! it hath a fiendish look"
(The Pilot made reply)—
"I am a-feared—" "Push on, push on!"
Said the Hermit cheerily.

Sample questions for the principal:

1. In the pilot's phrase "I trow," what does *trow* mean?
2. What does the Hermit mean when he says "by my faith"?

3. In the phrase "so thin and sere" what does *sere* mean?

4. How would the clause "that lag my forest-brook along" read without the inversion?

5. What does *lag* mean in that clause?

6. What is the "ivy-tod"?

7. What type of sentence is the sentence from "Unless . . . . young."? And what are its clauses?

8. In the Pilot's phrase "it hath a fiendish look" what does *fiendish* mean?

9. In what specific ways is the appearance of the mariner's ship similar to the appearance of the scene the Hermit describes?

10. Why doesn't the strange appearance of the ship alarm the Hermit as it does the Pilot?

Though this particular type of oral lesson is the staple of our vocabulary routine, we have tried numerous variations that encourage students to recognize and go beyond the limits of their understanding. Students may meet in groups of three and four to compare entries made for a particular passage and to resolve differences in understanding. This variation frequently presses the most able students to articulate precisely what they know about a word's denotation or connotation. A further variation is to have students exchange notebooks with a partner and devise a test for the other from the available entries. Still a third variation is to offer the students appropriate synonyms and synonymous phrases for words from the passage selected and to have them supply the author's word from their notebooks. No doubt there are other possibilities as well.

If the lessons we have described and illustrated are less like "vocabulary lessons" and more like what the French call *explication des textes,* that is because the explication approach properly subordinates word study to the larger aims of the English program and thus generates students' attention and effort. This sort of word study helps the student to cultivate a sense for *le mot juste* that is indispensable for writing development and to understand and appreciate the literature being read. In fact, in helping the student to overcome "inattention to words" (which Mortimer Adler, in *How to Read a Book,* calls the worst fault of the passive reader), this approach to vocabulary fosters appreciation. Both spontaneous expressions of admiration for the aptness of a writer's word choice and earnest questions about the meaning or purpose of word choice are the frequent responses to the oral recitation lesson. This is an approach, then, that does not shorten the time devoted to reading and writing instruction since it is an integral part of that instruction.

Finally, we offer this approach because it rewards effort, it accommodates the large differences in verbal sophistication that exist among students, and it recognizes that the simple, more familiar word, especially when it is used figuratively, may present just as much difficulty for students as does the so-called big word. These advantages of the program and the fact that it is easy to administer and sustain lift a great burden off the English teacher's back.

Notes

1. Rollo Brown, *How the French Boy Learns to Write* (Cambridge, Mass.: Harvard University Press, 1963), p. 49.

2. Ibid., pp. 49–50.

Teaching Word-Building Skills

Leslie Anne Hollingsworth
Inglewood High School, California

Are you and your students turned-off by the monotony of teacher-generated vocabulary lists? Are you concerned about the minimal retention students demonstrate when evaluated on the meanings of words they have supposedly "mastered" from these lists? Are you interested in insuring that your students develop the skills necessary to increase their vocabularies on their own, in addition to vocabulary enrichment accomplished through the use of teacher-selected words? Are you intrigued with the possibility of having your students share your excitement for words as "words"? This article explains how students can succeed in developing their vocabularies.

In my tenth-grade English classes, my students are offered a year-long structured program for developing word-building skills. At the beginning of the year, I start with a simple activity, such as giving students a long word(s) (for example, name of the high school, name of an upcoming holiday or event) from which they find and write as many shorter words as possible. This activity gets students interested in the idea that words can be fun to play with. Subsequent lessons involve the study of (1) syllabication, (2) abbreviations, (3) synonyms, antonyms, homonyms, and heteronyms, (4) context clues, and (5) prefixes, suffixes, and roots. In accelerated classes, I also include etymology, acronyms, euphemisms, and trade names that have become generic terms.

The first fifteen to twenty minutes of one class period, one day per week are devoted to vocabulary-building skills. All information is written on the board. Discussion of a particular word-building skill includes its relevance to the student, a review of previous material, and the meanings and/or structure of words given as examples. Students take notes to use in studying for future quizzes.

A contest follows discussion. The contest format varies, but in general each student is asked to apply the skill discussed by writing as many words as possible within a four- to five-minute time limit. During this time I circulate among students monitoring progress and offering encouragement. After "time" has been called, the total number of words each student has created is placed at the top of the paper. The two or three students with the highest word totals read their lists aloud. After each reading, students and teacher may challenge whether a word is actually a word or whether the spelling is accurate. Use of a dictionary dispels any controversy and encourages students to use this basic resource. The student who has the highest number of words is the contest winner and earns extra-credit points, which are added to the student's regular point total at the end of each quarter. Vocabulary papers are occasionally collected by the teacher to monitor progress but are usually kept by the students so that they don't have the feeling that everything they do will be red-penciled by the teacher. The contest motivates students by competition and by the possibility of receiving extra credit. Further, it involves the application of skills and immediate knowledge of results.

After a few lessons on each component of the program (for example, prefixes), students review the material orally. Attention and participation are thereby encouraged by the prospect of receiving additional extra-credit points for contributing to the discussion. A written quiz evaluates each student's ability to remember meanings and definitions of words discussed in class and to apply this knowledge by generating "new" words and by ascertaining the meanings of unfamiliar words.

The following is a specific example of a vocabulary-building skill lesson on suffixes. This information is put on the board:

Vocabulary-Suffixes

1. Review:
   Purpose
   Definition
   Words from last week: sense*less*, perish*able*, vigor*ous*

2. New Material: journa*list*, predica*ment*, procrastina*tion*
   (Questions asked include:
   How is the word pronounced?
   What is the suffix?
   What is the meaning of the whole word?
   What is the meaning of the suffix?
   What part of speech results from the use of all three of these suffixes?)

3. Contest: Write as many words as you can from the suffixes given below:

   -ist   -ment   -tion

There are many advantages in structuring a word-building skills program as I've described it: it provides variety within a class period; it generates active student participation; it decreases teacher-time spent dittoing and correcting papers; and, most importantly, it inspires students to develop the basic skills necessary to expand their own vocabularies.

6 Structuring Reading and the Teaching of Literature

Free Reading and Individualized Reading Instruction: A Successful Combination for the Middle School

Richard F. Abrahamson
University of Houston

The terms free reading and individualized reading are often used interchangeably even though they are not synonymous. Free reading is a term frequently used by high school English teachers to designate programs in which students select their own reading materials; individualized reading, on the other hand, is a term often used by elementary school teachers to designate a method of reading instruction in grades one through five. Oddly enough, the students who might benefit most from the two procedures are not in elementary school or in high school; rather, they are the middle school youngsters in grades five through eight. Unfortunately, unless their teachers were specifically trained to teach in the middle school, the teachers are unlikely to be familiar with both techniques. Some teachers may have picked up the idea of free reading as high school teachers and others may have received training in individualized reading techniques as elementary school instructors, but few will have mastered both techniques. What follows is a practical method for integrating free reading with individualized reading instruction in today's middle schools, but a fuller explanation of the two techniques must precede this discussion.

Free Reading as an Instructional Technique

Free reading began in the 1920s and had its first large-scale use in the 1930s under the direction of Dr. Lou LaBrant.[1] Essentially, students are given time in English class to read books of their own choosing. The program differs from Friday Free Reading because students read self-selected books during an entire course. Proponents of this approach argue that students in such programs read more and develop more positive attitudes toward books and reading than do students in traditional one-book-for-all programs.

Essential to the program is a series of conferences that provide time for the student to discuss with the teacher the most recently read book.

145

These conferences allow the teacher to assess how well a student has read a given book. Can the student discuss characterization? Can he or she compare one book with another or with a movie? Can the student discuss point of view and style? Is he or she aware of and able to talk about theme, setting, and the author's use of symbolism? These conferences, of course, emphasize reader reaction to a book, but they are also diagnostic in the sense that they encourage youngsters to respond critically as well as emotionally to books that they themselves have selected. The conclusion of the conference is always emphasized: the teacher looks at what the student likes to read, has read, and wishes to read and then suggests additional titles. For the teacher who is knowledgeable about books, this moment represents a powerful opportunity for reading guidance. The student who loves mystery stories may have read the Nancy Drew books but be encouraged through teacher suggestions to move up the reading ladder from Nancy Drew to Joan Lowery Nixon's *The Kidnapping of Christina Lattimore* to Henry James's *The Turn of the Screw.*

Studies show that students in free-reading programs do indeed read more books than do students in traditional English classes.[2] Perhaps more important is their attitude toward reading and books. Comments from teachers and students almost invariably point to the high level of student enthusiasm for books and for reading as a result of free-reading programs. Perhaps the greatest testament is found in Dr. LaBrant's follow-up study of students who participated in her free-reading program of 1936: *twenty-five years later* those students "were doing significantly more reading than most other groups with which they were compared."[3]

Individualized Reading Instruction

Teacher education courses in elementary reading often present individualized reading instruction as an alternative to teaching reading with a basal series.[4] As it is typically described, individualized reading instruction has five steps. Motivation, the first step, is tied closely to classroom environment: reading materials must be available. Books, posters, magazines, and printed matter of all kinds need to be readily available. A recent study by Janet Hickman found that more reading takes place when a library of books is available in the classroom itself—even if the school library is only a few steps away.[5] The next step, student selection of materials, parallels a major tenet of free-reading programs. Students are free to choose what they want to read and to use class time to do that reading. The third step is a conference during which the student reads aloud from the book he or she has chosen and the teacher asks questions about the student's response to the book along with questions about plot, setting, characterization, and the like. While the fourth step is an outgrowth of the third, many see it as the center of individualized reading instruction. As the student reads aloud, the teacher notes reading strengths and weaknesses. Perhaps the student needs help with initial consonant blends or is failing to use context clues. On the basis of this reading diagnosis, the student is placed in a small group that works in common on assigned skills, or the teacher may assign individual work covering particular skills. The fifth and final step involves peer reaction and follow-up activities that center on the books read. In place of the standard book report, students are encouraged to respond to books in other ways. They might dramatize part of a book, illustrate another, or correspond with the author of a third. The important point is to encourage students to respond creatively to books.

While free reading and individualized reading share the goal of producing students who enjoy reading, the initial intent of each is different. Their current separation—one as a reading instruction technique in the elementary classroom and the other as a teaching strategy in the high school English class—is perhaps indicative of a larger problem in the teaching of reading and English. Students in English classes often do not see exercises in reading instruction as related to reading enjoyable books. Reading tends to be looked upon as a subject to be studied like math, while reading books for pleasure is something quite different. Indeed, to many youngsters the two appear to be mutually exclusive activities. Although reading instruction ought to show youngsters why they might want to read, free reading cannot take place unless students know how to read. By combining free reading and individualized reading techniques, teachers are able to work within a single framework to help their students develop reading skills and the ability to analyze what they read.

Combining Instructional Techniques in the Middle School

The middle school teacher is often faced with students who need instruction in basic reading skills as well as instruction in literary terms and critical reading. Additionally, some students are poorly motivated readers and may need the freedom of selection to encourage them to read. As a result, the middle school classroom, where students look back to reading instruction and move forward to more mature literary analysis, may represent the ideal setting in which to combine the techniques of free reading and individualized reading instruction.

For a trial period of instruction combining the two techniques, the middle school teacher should plan a three-week initial unit. Teachers who begin individualized reading programs often complain about the record keeping and paper work, and those who start free-reading programs complain about the number of books they must read or skim; thus the three-week interval is a good testing period for the teacher and still allows students the necessary free-reading time to complete some self-selected books. An inventory of reading interests should be administered to get some sense of each student's reading preferences and to enable the teacher to make appropriate book suggestions. Favorite TV shows, movies, hobbies, sports, books, and magazines are all helpful clues in suggesting appropriate books.

In a middle school that designates a specific scope and sequence of reading skills, such guidelines help define what to look for during the student-teacher conference. Those teachers free to develop their own reading skills list may be guided by the following scope and sequence of skills suggested by Martha Dillner and Joanne Olson.

1. Using Illustration Clues
2. Using Context Clues
3. Using Phonic Analysis
4. Using Structural Analysis
5. Using Dictionary Skills
6. Expanding Background in Vocabulary
7. Using a Combination of Vocabulary Skills
8. Identifying Details
9. Identifying Main Ideas
10. Identifying Sequence
11. Following Directions
12. Identifying Cause-Effect Relationships
13. Making Inferences
14. Making Generalizations and Conclusions
15. Identifying Tone and Mood
16. Identifying Theme
17. Identifying Characterization
18. Identifying Fact, Fiction, and Opinion
19. Identifying Propaganda
20. Identifying Author's Purpose
21. Scheduling Time
22. Setting Purposes
23. Using a Study Technique
24. Using Locational Aids in the Library
25. Recording References
26. Using the Library Call System
27. Using Locational Aids Within Books
28. Using Footnotes
29. Using Glossaries
30. Using Maps, Graphs, and Tables
31. Matching Materials with Purposes
32. Understanding the Organization of Paragraphs
33. Organizing Information
34. Adjusting Rate to Purpose[6]

Most of these skills are applicable to a work of fiction; also, students are free to choose nonfiction titles, in which case all these skills could be checked, diagnosed, and taught as needed.

Students in this three-week course select their reading materials and read during class. After finishing a book, each student signs up for a ten-to fifteen-minute conference with the teacher and selects a short passage that he or she finds especially important or well written to read aloud to the teacher. Aside from skills using context clues, phonic analysis, and structural analysis (numbers 2, 3, and 4 on the above list), the teacher is able to assess students' skills through questions, so the reading aloud portion of the conference can be eliminated for any students who have no difficulty with those three reading skills.

Obviously, not every reading skill is going to be covered in every reading conference, and not every book lends itself to each of the listed skills. Perhaps two reading skills might be integrated with several literary concerns. Specific questions about setting, theme, style, and so forth can be posed to the student, who should have some freedom to focus on one or two aspects of literature that seem most pertinent to the particular book read.

In the last few years much has been written about levels of questions and responses to literature. There typically is not enough time to structure specific questions about every book read in such a program. Accordingly, teachers develop general sets of questions on characterization, theme, and style, and students relate these questions to the specific work. One set of questions—developed by Richard Peck, the author of young-adult novels—takes into account the media-saturated lives of our students and also provides room for individual response to literature while still requiring a careful look at the text itself.

1. What would this story be like if the main character were of the opposite sex?
2. Why is this story set where it is (not *what* is the setting)?
3. If you were to film this story, what characters would you eliminate if you couldn't use them all?
4. Would you film this story in black and white or in color?
5. How is the main character different from you?
6. Why or why not would this story make a good TV series?
7. What's one thing in this story that's happened to you?
8. Reread the first paragraph of Chapter 1. What's in it that makes you read on?
9. If you had to design a new cover for this book, what would it look like?
10. What does the title tell you about the book? Does it tell the truth?[7]

When the student finishes this conference combining the demonstration of reading skills and the discussion of literary aspects, the teacher has valuable information about which reading skills need to be developed and what aspects of literature should be probed for in future conferences. All this is done using materials selected by the student; the combination of instructional techniques has enhanced reading skills and literary skills and has led to enjoyable reading.

Evaluating Students in the Combined Instructional Program

There are several techniques for assigning letter grades to students in the combined instructional system just described. The most frequently used grading system is described in an article by Bruce Appleby and John Conner.

1. Number of books read. This measure *alone* is unreliable in that books vary so greatly in length and difficulty. Nevertheless, students have always felt that quantity of reading is important.

2. Number of books read is multiplied by an estimate of the student's perceptiveness of what he or she has read. The student is graded on the student-teacher conference on a cumulative scale of 1 to 4: 1–no understanding beyond plot; 2–some application to the student's life; 3–some implications for larger human ideas; 4–understanding of levels of meaning, esthetic values, and relationships with other reading.

3. The product of criteria one and two is multiplied by an estimate of the level of the book. Each book is given a numerical rating on a scale of 1 to 4: 1–Adolescent; 2–Popular Adult; 3–Serious Adult; 4–Classic.[8]

The authors point out that the scale can be adjusted according to ability group and grade level. For example, a book that might be "serious adult" for a seventh grader might be "popular adult" for a twelfth grader. Further, a student who reads and understands completely an "adolescent" book may achieve as high a grade as another student who has a lower level of understanding of a "serious adult" book. In the combined program described, the middle school teacher would also assign a reading skill improvement grade that would be determined over a longer period of time, not at the end of every conference.

Conclusion

The combining of free reading and individualized reading provides middle school teachers with a structure that allows them to teach reading skills and the analysis of literature while working with student-selected reading materials and individual responses to those materials. Integrating these approaches enables teachers to provide some guidance as they suggest other books to read; it creates a climate for good student-teacher rapport in the sharing of opinions about books. The structure of this teaching method makes it possible for students to progress at their own rate, so great variations in reading levels and interests can be accommodated. How encouraging to think that this approach might influence students to see a common link between reading skills and pleasure reading and to read for the pure joy of it in later life.

Notes

1. Lou LaBrant, *An Evaluation of the Free Reading in Grades Ten, Eleven, and Twelve,* Ohio State University Studies, Contributions to Education, no. 2 (Columbus: Ohio State University Press, 1936).

2. Harrison J. Means, "Nine Years of Individualized Reading," *Journal of Reading* 20 (November 1976): 144-49.

3. Lou LaBrant, "The Use of Communication Media," in *The Guinea Pigs after Twenty Years,* ed. Margaret Willis (Columbus: Ohio State University, 1961), pp. 127-64.

4. The following two books are noteworthy for their treatment of individualized reading instruction: Jeannette Veatch, *Reading in the Elementary School* (New York: Wiley, 1978)—this fine resource on individualized reading instruction is filled with specific suggestions for implementing the program; and Barbara Blow, *Individualized Reading—A Course of Study* (Cedar Falls, Iowa, 1974)—the most complete guide available on how to structure an individualized reading program, the book includes conference questions, handouts, and grading procedures. (For ordering information, write to Barbara Blow, 1701 Waterlow Road, Cedar Falls, Iowa 50613.)

5. Janet G. Hickman, "Reponse to Literature in a School Environment, Grades K–5" (Ph.D. diss., Ohio State University, 1979).

6. Martha H. Dillner and Joanne P. Olson, *Personalizing Reading Instruction in Middle, Junior, and Senior High Schools* (New York: Macmillan, 1977), p. 229.

7. Richard Peck, "Ten Questions to Ask about a Novel," *The ALAN Newsletter* 5 (Spring 1978): 1 and 7.

8. Bruce C. Appleby and John W. Conner, "Well, What Did You Think of It?" *English Journal* 54 (October 1965): 610.

A February Gimmick

Betty Ann Fargnoli
Quabbin Regional High School, Barre, Massachusetts

Scene I: "English Teacher in Dreamland"

Time: 5:30 A.M.

Place: Room 318, Modern High School, Anywhere, U.S.A.

(Students enter English classroom quietly, open neatly kept notebooks as they sit at shining desks, eagerly awaiting accustomed pearls of wisdom that regularly fall from the lips of Ms. English Teacher, hereafter known as ME.)

> ME: Thank you, students, for your usual prompt attention and total silence following the bell. I know you will be happy to learn that today we shall begin our new poetry unit.

(Students cheer, quietly, of course.)

> Student #1: Hurrah!
>
> Student #2: Oh, good! I've been waiting all term for this.
>
> Student #3: Thanks, Ms. English Teacher, for coming up with another great unit idea!

(Just as I am about to bow to the Students' standing ovation, I hear the peal of my alarm clock.)

Scene II: "English Teacher in Realityland"

Time: 8:45 A.M.

Place: Same as in Scene I

(Students enter Room 318 in high agitation. They are angry or upset about: (a) a new demerit system; (b) an old demerit system; (c) loss of privileges; (d) all of the above; (e) something else.)

> ME: All right, class, quiet down. Good news. We have completed all of the departmental curriculum objectives for *The Great Gatsby*.

(Sounds of book being handed to front of room amid loud cheers.)

> ME: O.K., quiet down, please! We've "done" the short story, the novel, and the essay. Now it's time to "do" poetry.
>
> Student #1: Boo! Hiss!
>
> Student #2: I hate poetry!
>
> Student #3: Give *Gatsby* back! (I've never heard from *him* before.)
>
> Student #4: Let me out of here.
>
> Student #5: Can I go to the bathroom?
>
> All: When does this period get over?

(Sounds of teacher gritting teeth and digging in for a long battle.)

English teachers may teach structure in the novel, the elements of the short story, composition, syntax, sentence combining, and, sometimes, when pressured, grammar. But what is nearest and dearest to an English teacher's heart is poetry. And, unfortunately, what is furthest from the hearts of and most despised by high school English students is poetry. The methods of teaching poetry that I have attempted include:

> lecture
>
> small group work
>
> reader's theater
>
> multiple texts
>
> student reports
>
> "Rock lyrics really are poetry."
>
> "Let's go to the library and find a poet."
>
> mass hypnosis

All of these techniques have met with some measure of success, and I'll probably use most of them again, depending upon the level of the class, the time of the year, and the waxing of the moon. But for now, on a gloomy February morning, I need a new idea, another approach, a gimmick, if you will.

Here is a "February (or March, or June) Gimmick." It has worked for me for three years. If my good fortune continues, I'll get another year or two out of it. To you, *bona fortuna.*

Like many English teachers, I once took something called Modern Poetry in grad school and was informed that modern American poetry began in 1912, etc. But we know that it really began with our old friends Walt Whitman and Emily Dickinson, those iconoclastic experimenters who somehow got lost in the wrong century, not to mention being among the missing in my too short fall semester. Before I stifle the moans, groans, and muttered curses of my class and command them to open the Sacred Text, I turn (often in desperation) to some of Emily's riddle poems. I have prepared overhead transparencies of the following poems:

"A Narrow Fellow in the Grass"

"I Like to See It Lap the Miles"

"It Sifts from Leaden Sieves"

"A Route of Evanescence"

"I Never Lost as Much but Twice"

"My Life Closed Twice Before Its Close"

This list is not based on any particularly esoteric educational theory other than a gradual movement from the concrete to the abstract plus personal choice.

After reading the poem, the class guesses as to the riddle poem's hidden subject and the responses are written on the blackboard. When we have from three to five possibilities, I ask the students if any of their guesses are illogical in the context of the poet's time, such as a jet plane or motorcycle race (after all, I point out, Emily died in 1886). Often the list of guesses can be pared down to two. Now, those students who volunteered what appear to be "correct guesses" attempt to prove their theories, aided and abetted by their supporters. Eventually, only one theory remains, one that has been supported by evidence. The class has been introduced to and given a practical lesson in textual analysis, and it hardly hurt at all. We continue in this fashion through the easier (concrete) poems, with me often playing Devil's Advocate.

Finally, we tackle the more difficult (abstract) riddle poems. Naturally, it is harder to narrow the guesses down to just one. But that's all right because students know that even though there may be more than one interpretation of a poem, each interpretation must be backed by hard, supporting evidence and not just unsubstantiated feelings or emotions. Other outcomes of this exercise include, but are not limited to, student discovery of such poetic conventions as:

imagery patterns

similes and metaphors

structure and stanza variations

punctuation and capitalization variations

allusions

tone

patterns of rhythm and meter

diction and its special importance in poetry

Best of all, I have not resorted to lecture, reader's theater, rock lyrics, or hypnosis. The class has done it all; I have simply functioned as scribe and referee. And I actually have everyone's attention turned in a fairly positive attitude toward poetry.

If you wish to go a step further, the class can now produce their own riddle poems. After the initial cries of anguish from the complainers, the folded-arms, rigid-back syndrome from the downright hostile, and the attempts to make eye contact with the students who have just finished the creative writing elective from the politicians, I soothe the ruffled feathers with the information that this will be a group effort and that students may remain anonymous authors if they wish. In practice, they are usually quite willing to claim credit for their masterpieces later.

How teachers manage small group work is an individual preference, but I do suggest setting time limits for the following activities:

finding a topic/theme

free writing, listing, brainstorming, etc.

first draft

second draft

final touches before transcribing onto overhead transparencies

I also make the following suggestions to the class:

Begin your riddle poem in the concrete and then move to the abstract. (They may remain with the concrete if they wish.)

As I move about and talk with each group, I remind them of what they have learned from Emily about poetic compression so that they will weed out the extra words (some of which would give away the riddle too easily and spoil the game).

I encourage any and all flights of fancy and sometimes suggest an attempt at "patterned" or shaped poetry. This has worked especially well with riddle poems that describe the flight of a frisbee (an always popular topic) or this year's favorite, hang-gliding. It also gives me the opportunity to introduce the twentieth-century version, typographical poetry, as well as John Ciardi's concept of "How Does a Poem Mean?"

The final step, of course, is the class's attempt to guess the riddle poems produced by their colleagues when displayed on the overhead projector.

I would not state categorically that this gimmick will produce a scene bearing any resemblance whatsoever to Scene I: "English Teacher in Dreamland," but the class and I have at least eased our way into poetry, and the reader's theater, lectures on prosody and figures of speech, student reports, and other coming attractions may just possibly go a little smoother this year.

Writer Role Playing:
An Alternative to the Book Report
and the Five-Paragraph Theme

Charles I. Schuster
University of Washington

In the past, I have been able to teach literature and get exciting readings and to teach composition and get exciting writings—but seldom have I been able to get both in one course. In despair, I hit upon a strategy that may help other literature teachers in various grade levels take increasing delight in their students' essays.

The despair—and the enlightenment—surfaced in a recent course I taught to college sophomores entitled "Popular Literature." Most of the students were non-English majors, intelligent, dimly interested, but unschooled as close readers. My intent was to teach them the forms of fiction, using science fiction as the mode.

We began with H. G. Wells's *War of the Worlds,* a splendid novel because it is a story well told by a quirky narrator, fascinating in his own right. I offered my students two topics—one on the narrator, the other on the novel in its philosophical setting. The specific assignments were as follows:

> We have already talked a bit about narration. This novel is told through a first person narration. Using suitable passages from the text, define and describe the narrator. What kind of a man is he? What is his profession? Is he likable? How would you describe his character and personality?

> Like so many writers in the nineteenth and twentieth centuries, Wells was greatly influenced by Darwin and the theory of evolution. In what ways does this novel reveal and reflect the impact of evolutionary theory? What does the novel suggest about "survival of the fittest"? Who (or what) are the fittest? Is the novel in any way ironic? Use passages from the text to support your view.

My students wrote dutiful responses. Generally they said: *"War of the Worlds* is a fascinating novel, but what is most interesting is the narrator. As revealed by the novel, the narrator is . . ."* or *"War of the Worlds* is a fascinating novel, but what is most interesting is the way it is influenced by Darwin and the theory of evolution. As revealed by the novel, evolu-

157

tion is . . . ." They were giving me exactly what I demanded of them: writing that was informative, dull, voiceless, formulaic, uninterested, and altogether uninteresting.

Two facts compounded this problem. The first was that I had fifty-seven students enrolled. The second was that I had already committed them to write—and me to read—an essay a week on each new novel. Given the three-page length of most responses and the ten-week quarter, I was looking forward to 1,710 pages plus the final exam by the end of March.

The students never complained about the dullness of my topics or the dullness of their writing. Sadly, they expected little else. Nor was I yet aware of the problem in any specific way. The second essay called for them to "define science fiction" by focusing on a few short stories; the third assignment was to produce a symbolic interpretation of *The Puppet Masters* by Robert A. Heinlein. The writing remained as perfunctory as ever, the five-paragraph theme reigning supreme. Their responses should not have surprised me; what I was asking them, after all, was to write to me about what I already knew, and what they knew that I already knew. My students were learning, I thought, but in a passive, unimaginative way. The contrast between their essays and the novels we were reading gnawed at the edges of my mind. Why couldn't their essays in some way recreate the drama of the novels we were reading?

In fact they could, but both the students and I were afraid to try. For the next novel, *The Forever War* by Joe Haldeman, I included an option that they think of themselves as "the lone Tauran survivor of Aleph Aurigae and write a report about the attack to the other Taurans." My students preferred instead to analyze the military as presented by the novel or to compare the book to *The Puppet Masters*. None chose to become Tauran for a day. To attempt such an essay involved risks that no one wanted to take. The graded weekly essays determined their final grade; no one wished to jeopardize their grade point average just to inhabit the Tauran consciousness. Better to play it safe—and dull—with the standard analytic or comparative essay.

The crisis occurred when neither they nor I could play it safe. We had read Arthur C. Clarke's *Childhood's End,* a moving, lucid novel, so lucid in fact that I could think of nothing to pose as an essay question. The novel explicates itself; it leaves no literary stone unturned. In desperation, I offered only two choices:

> You are now in your forties, a parent, and your child is three years old. Your child starts to change, to transform in the manner described by the novel. Express what it is you feel about the change. How do you feel about your child, the world, yourself, the human race?

> You are a child, nine years old. You are beginning to change in the manner suggested by *Childhood's End.* Write a description of this change, describing what you feel. How is your perception changing? What do you feel about the earth, your parents, yourself, the human race?

Actually, the two assignments represent only one choice: inhabit a role and write from within the fictional context supplied by the novel.

The responses were insightful and even moving. For a short interval, many of the students became both character and author, both reader and writer. Just as importantly, their responses indicated the ways they understood the novel as narrative form, as statement about parent and child, as patterning of image and meaning. Their essays contained many allusions to other characters and events in the novel; more importantly, most of them captured the elegiac optimism of the narrative that mourns the death of the human race while simultaneously celebrating its transformation into a higher order of existence.

Subsequent assignments asked students to write a three-page excerpt from *The Theory of Social Entropy,* a nonexistent study cited frequently in *Agent of Chaos* by Norman Spinrad, and to compose a dialogue between two Gethenians, "one who considers alien human beings to be 'perverts' and dangerous, another who believes that alien humans and the Ekumen represent Gethen's best hope" (*Left Hand of Darkness* by Ursula K. LeGuin). In each case, the responses offered useful syntheses of the novel. The dialogue assignment, in particular, compelled students to place themselves within the context of the novel and to grapple with one of the philosophic questions at its center.

What I am suggesting here is that we not only encourage but actually compel our students to write within the framework of fiction in the literature we teach. This is not the same as asking them to become creative writers. Our goal is not to make them into novelists or poets, but to induce them to participate imaginatively in literature while simultaneously grounding them within the text. In effect, this technique asks them to become both participants and spectators. According to James Britton:

> When we use language to recount or recreate real or imagined experience for no other reason than to enjoy it or present it for enjoyment, we are using language in the role of spectator; when we use language to get things done, we are in the role of participants (participants in "the world's affairs"). The latter role includes the use of language to recount or recreate real or imagined experience in order to inform or teach, or to make plans or solicit help or to achieve any other practical outcome.[1]

Most essays about literature are written purely to restate information that the teacher already knows with a minimum of involvement on the part of the writer. However, role-playing assignments move the writer toward the pure pleasure of the spectator while urging the writer to be participant as well. That is, the students delight in creating fictions within fictions while making themselves and their readers aware of formal, literal, and symbolic meanings in the text.

Writer role playing proved to be no pedagogical quirk. Recently I asked students on a midterm to "write the response that Pippip [*The Death Ship* by B. Traven] would make if he read Flaubert's 'A Simple Heart.' Use his voice or your own, but write from his viewpoint about Felicite's life and its meaning." In addition, my students answered questions that required them to explain the philosophic significance of Jean Paul Sartre's "The Wall" and to analyze the theme of betrayal in *Red Harvest* by Dashiell Hammett. In discussing the midterm afterward, they acclaimed the role-playing question as the most enjoyable and illuminating; their answers bore this out. In "becoming Pippip," my students learned that magical concept called inhabiting a text. They became readers who write what they read. They internalized the text without necessarily having to make their knowledge explicit. They performed the text, producing for themselves and for the reader pleasure in the doing and in the thing done.

Writer role playing is not a frivolous activity. It represents an attempt to bring play and expressiveness into the classroom. John Dixon has written that "Play has long been recognized as an essential part of work in the best primary schools; what we need now is an increased awareness of the language purposes it encourages and develops."[2] Play is important at all levels as a way of engaging a problem, solving it creatively, and interacting with texts and ideas. James Britton, Janet Emig, and others have argued persuasively for the importance of the expressive-reflexive mode of writing. Writer role playing is exploratory and close to the self in precisely the ways they advocate. Finally, such writing allows students to synthesize and theorize. When I ask my students to inhabit the role of a particular novelist and produce an alternate ending to a book we have read, they think through assumptions about this novel in particular and all novels in general. They are led to think about foreshadowing, the inevitability of plot and character, and the poetic rightness of various conclusions. They give me the unexpected because it is impossible for them to reproduce lecture or discussion. Their written responses range far beyond classroom context so that they gain the possibility of intellectual independence.

Essays produced through writer role playing can be graded or ungraded like any others. Grading criteria may be based on involvement within the role, embodiment of ideas, organization, rhetorical effectiveness, and engagement with the primary text. If anything, these kinds of essays enlarge the narrow perspective of most evaluators: instead of looking for the thesis sentence, linear development of an argument, and reasonableness of conclusion, role-playing essays can be evaluated on the basis of their conception, effectiveness, engagement, and originality.

Writer role playing can be an exciting addition to an introductory literature class, be it second grade or a sophomore survey course. In combination with the more traditional assignments, role-playing essays improve understanding, allowing teachers and students to become collaborative learners in the classroom. As a way of defining and structuring a reading class, this approach can produce magical consequences—excited readers and exciting writing.

Notes

1. James Britton et al., *The Development of Writing Abilities (11-18)* (London: Macmillan Education, 1975), pp. 92-93.

2. John Dixon, *Growth through English,* 3rd ed. (Oxford: Oxford University Press, 1975), p. 25.

Possessing the Origins of Literature

Don Austin
Lincoln High School, Portland, Oregon

Have you practiced so long to learn to read?
Have you felt so proud to get at the meaning of poems?

Stop this day and night with me and you shall possess the origin of
all poems,
You shall possess the good of the earth and sun, (there are millions
of suns left,)
You shall no longer take things at second or third hand, nor look
through the eyes of the dead, nor feed on the spectres in books,
You shall not look through my eyes either, nor take things from me,
You shall listen to all sides and filter them from yourself.

Walt Whitman

In our classroom worship of great literature, we often do our students an intellectual disservice by teaching them to look through the eyes of the dead, by taking things secondhand and thirdhand, and by requiring that they use a deadening critical approach. To paraphrase Emerson, why should they not also enjoy an original relation to literature? Why should they not also have a poetry of insight and not of tradition imposed upon them by secondary English teachers anxious to get the interpretation right?

Most of us who went through college during the 50s, 60s, and 70s had heavy doses of the "New Criticism"—explication of the text, focus on the work itself, Allen Tate, Robert Penn Warren, and all that. Many of us swallowed the textual analysis approach whole as the only way of looking at literature in the high school. A scene from Andy Warhol's film *High School* in which students groan or remain silent through the dissection of a Simon and Garfunkel song comes to mind, reminding me that during the "Soft Revolution" phase of the late 60s and early 70s, even the "hip" teachers hung onto the old critical tools, though we found new meat to cut up.

Although it may sound like it, this is not a blast at the "New Criticism," which has given us many new insights into literature we would otherwise lack. Students who are ready for it, especially advanced students thinking of taking the literature advanced placement test, can learn a great deal about writing and literature through explicating poems and using the elements of fiction to interpret novels. Yet there must be more in the teacher's approach to literary criticism than Robert Penn Warren. By using a series of writing assignments that progressively take the student deeper into the ideas and techniques of a work, we can help students see literature through their own eyes, writing about it as something close to them that they possess.

The sequence of assignments that follows parallels what Moffett, Britton, and Macrorie have long said should be done in teaching writing in order to guarantee quality writing from the start: begin with the student writers' recent personal experiences, then move gradually toward more abstract and distant topics. Piaget's ideas on intellectual growth can be applied to students' writing about literature. Begin with the students' gut responses to the work; then, through the course of a school year or several school years, move toward impressionistic reponses; then social, historical, and psychological approaches; and finally the more abstract textual analysis, always finding specific things in the work for them to focus on. Although some traditionalists may squirm at the thought of fourteen-year-olds condemning *A Midsummer Night's Dream* or *The Adventures of Huckleberry Finn,* this approach is not aimed at their comfort. It is meant to help students enjoy and understand literature, to "filter" from themselves.

In *A Vulnerable Teacher,* Ken Macrorie describes what happens when the teacher allows students to respond to the literature in any way they want by keeping a journal and from time to time exploring their insights further with revisions. Students learn to think for themselves, to trust one another, and to explore with detail whatever response they may have to a book. Dittoing sample responses from a class and discussing what a student has written and how it was written can be far more valuable than reading what a critic has said, since the critic is not there to discuss views.

Richard Adler also has an innovative approach to discussing students' first responses to a piece of literature, which has an interesting side effect of getting students deeper into the text than they generally would with a typical explication discussion. The teacher must refrain from making any judgment of the work and must lead a discussion in which students tell what their reaction is. Each reaction is recorded on the board. Without commenting on the reactions, the teacher allows students to share responses until they are through with the list. Next students pick one response to explore, divide into groups with others who have made the same choice, or work by themselves if they are the only one with a certain opinion. Directions are simply to go through the work with the group (or individual student) finding everything that makes them respond as they did. Then students share what they have uncovered, quoting lines from the text to illustrate their point of view. Often two opposing groups end up in an interesting disagreement that can be made into a regular debate the next day, resolution and all, with both sides having the right to come up with the most persuasive evidence. Symposia, role playing, TV talk shows with characters from the work, film scripts of scenes, short poems, or any other such forum from actual life enhances this approach, evoking honest responses and interest as well as laying a foundation of digging into the text for future literary studies.

After students are used to discussing their honest responses to what they read, it is time to move on to more specific methods of impressionistic response. The most obvious place from which to build is to have students do revisions of the Macrorie free-writing or the Adler responses; they should pay close attention that they specifically demonstrate their own point of view. In addition, David Bleich and James Moffett have some interesting approaches for getting students to discuss and understand what they are reading in some unusual, creative ways.

From Bleich I have gleaned the idea of having students choose the most important word, aspect, or passage from whatever they are reading. By beginning with a discussion or free writing and focusing on a portion of the text that is not too long, students are actually discussing more fundamental questions in literature and their own writing, such as "What is important in a work of literature or any writing?" as well as seeing the importance of word choice in writing. To improve their chances of forming a well-organized paragraph or essay response, the teacher can have students write a specific one-sentence statement of opinion, using it as a topic or thesis sentence. To emphasize specific development, the teacher can also have students list items that illustrate their point of view in their one-sentence response. In addition to writing more successfully about literature, students are getting deeper into the text from their points of view in an interesting and painless fashion.

Of all the writing assignments Moffett suggests, the ones I have found most successful with literature students are the monologue, dialogue, and diary. Each assignment requires students to use imagination to figure out how characters think and act, and their sensitive monologues and dialogues usually demonstrate that their understanding is more than just intellectual. With the monologue, the teacher tells students to become one of the characters they are studying and to write an interior thought monologue from that character's point of view, using the character's manner of thinking and expression. In order to make it a more creative assignment, the setting of their scene should be outside the actual work—between chapters, before or after the book—while the character thinks over what has happened to that point. The dialogue assignment is much the same, except students choose two characters who are in disagreement about something significant. What would the Puritan Jonathan Edwards have had to say to the libertine Ben Franklin? How did Hester Prynne handle telling Dimmesdale that he was about to become a father? The responses of my students to situations such as these show that they know the characters firsthand. The diary assignment is a bit tougher since the student must role play a character and keep a record of that person's reactions to what is going on daily in the text. With such assignments, students enjoy reading their contributions to the stories to the whole class.

"Real Life Reviews" is the next assignment I give, and this gets students thinking and backing up what they say with evidence. Since students are not generally experts on literature, and since we want them to write critiques as if they were experts, we ought to have them write about something in which they have expertise. A fourteen-year-old will rarely write as good a critical paragraph or essay about *The Rime of the Ancient Mariner* as about a swim meet or rock performance. For this assignment, students write a first-person essay on something they have experienced, something they know quite a bit about—a football game, concert, school policy or issue in the school paper, assembly, TV show, or some other sporting or entertainment event. They begin by jotting down notes, details, or ideas that someone "in the know" about the event would find worthy of praise or criticism. From this they develop a point of view around which to unify many or most of their ideas. Next they come up with as many concrete details that could be used to convince others of their point of view. Finally, they write a persuasive paragraph or essay that other students read before the teacher does, with all readers noting what is most convincing and what could be strengthened.

Toward the end of the school year, or in classes with more advanced students, I have found an adaptation of Pike and Young's tagmemic definition tools a successful method of getting students to understand characterization. According to Pike and Young, to know a thing one must see how it differs from other things similar to it (using the process of contrast), know where it fits into a range of similar things (classification), and see how it changes. This emphasis on contrast, classification, and change as definition tools has produced remarkable results in my classroom. With Warren's *All the King's Men,* students use a contrast free-write to compare the earlier Willie Stark to the later, Machiavellian one, citing specific examples from the text to support their contrasts. Later they write another fast-write in which they see where Stark fits into the range of all politicians, real and fictitious. Finally, when they are through with the book, they prepare one more free-write, delineating how Stark changes throughout the story. These free-writes become the basis of a character definition essay.

With advanced classes in Humanities, a year-long survey of world views in western civilization on the topics of art, literature, religion, music, and history, students have learned to think in ways I had never seen in previous classes that did not use the definition tools. Early in the year, I had them write three paragraph-length assignments on one character from *The Iliad,* each assignment using a different definition tool. Later, during a biblical unit, students began using the tools to examine contrasts in Greek and Hebrew concepts of God. Whenever possible, students were to use the definition tools to compare ideas from one culture to ideas of another, the object being that they would then be prone to use the tools in writing assignments. That object was realized, but another surprise was in store. Students began thinking and asking questions like advanced students in comparative literature: "What do the similarities and differences between Lancelot and Achilles tell us about their two cultures?" or, "How do differences in Dante's God and Milton's God (or Job's) show differences between cultural world views?"

For more advanced students, the Microcosm-Macrocosm assignment is an interesting variation on the contrast-classification-change writing discussed earlier. The assignment works best with certain works in which the micro-macro technique is used by the author: that is, in *The Tempest, Lord of the Flies,* or *The Stranger.* Students write an essay in which they show how a microcosm from the book parallels events in the macrocosm, concluding with comments on what the comparison suggests. Similarly students may choose something from actual life—school, marriage, athletics, an individual, city, relationship, or home situation—and show how this microcosm reflects a macrocosm—society, free enterprise, all humanity, politics, and so forth.

After some early failures with teaching literature, I am convinced that English teachers need to be trained more in ways of structuring a class to get students thinking about books than they need to know critical theories such as Burke's pentads or Frye's archetypes. Drama Groups and Fiction Panels are just such activities that take students deeper into literature while they are doing their own thinking.

The purposes of Drama Groups are to help students understand how characterization develops in a play and to help them be able to demonstrate that understanding with the text. During the study of a play, students are divided into groups, with each group specializing in a main character from the work. Each student stockpiles quotations from the play that help to develop an understanding of the motivation and personality of that character. During class discussions of the play, specialty groups are called upon to clarify their characters for the rest of the class. About halfway through the unit, students write an interior monologue, as described previously, and read their papers to the rest of the group, telling what they were trying to show about the character through the monologue. At the end of the unit, each group prepares and gives a short presentation to the class in which group members "define" their character using the earlier "definition tools" to show how their character develops in the play, contrasts with other characters, and ties in with the theme. Each group reads its best monologues aloud.

The Fiction Panel is similar in that students divide into specialty groups, though this time each group works with one of the elements of fiction in a novel (plot, character, setting, atmosphere, structure, symbolism) as that element develops the theme. The teacher must be careful in selecting a novel for study so that each group will have enough to work on. *The Scarlet Letter, The American, The Great Gatsby, The Adventures of Huckleberry Finn, All the King's Men, Wuthering Heights,* and *Great Expectations* have all proven successful. If the teacher would prefer shorter fiction, *The Norton Anthology to Literature* or *Contemporary American Short Stories* are ideal texts.

As with the Drama Groups, students stockpile textual material pertinent to the group topic, meeting once or twice during the unit to share findings and their implications. During these discussions, students identify problems they are having, phrasing them as questions that they can free write on to develop ideas. By the end of the unit, each individual is to have written a paper dealing with a specific aspect of the group's element of fiction and how it develops the theme in the book. Students are encouraged to develop different angles and use different portions of the text in order to make the group's investigation thorough. When the papers are done, students read them aloud in their groups, receiving positive comments and "specific improvement" critiques that they may use in revising for their final draft. For the panel presentation, students may read one or two of the strongest papers aloud to the entire class and discuss what they found out as a panel. Other students may also wish to ask questions, especially if they know they will be taking a short answer exam on how each element of fiction develops the theme in the novel being studied.

Both specialty group assignments can be adapted so that students focus on other items that the teacher wants to emphasize. In fact, all of the approaches discussed here are most effective when adapted to fit the individual teacher's personality, interests, and objectives.

Basic assumptions about life and teaching are hard to see and harder to change when change is desired. English teachers have long held the assumptions that writing was something students did for the teacher to correct so that the student could "get better" or, similarly, that literature was something to be explained so that students could understand and appreciate it. Both assumptions give the teacher the largest role and overlook writing, discussing, and reading as intellectual growth tools for students. If teachers truly want students to think and learn, they should use approaches that take the students from passively receiving ideas to thinking for themselves and from subjective and hazy reactions to more objective and thoughtful response.

Before lecturing on literature or dissecting your next poem in class, remember two things. First, students are people growing in language capabilities and need activities to develop their potential. And second,

> Surgeons must be very careful
> When they take the knife!
> Underneath their fine incisions
> Stirs the Culprit—Life!

> Emily Dickinson

Poetry: An Old Key to Open New Doors for Basic Skills Students

Violet Asmuth
Edison Community College, Fort Myers, Florida

Several articles have recently stressed that poetry units with special emphasis on minority poets and oral interpretation can be used to capture the interest of students enrolled in basic skills courses. Generally speaking, however, the idea seems not to have caught on. By way of contrast, those of us who teach in a CETA Youth Employability and Tutorial Program based in Fort Myers, Florida, have found the strategy highly successful. Our program, designed to raise grade levels in arithmetic, reading, and language arts, enrolls a new group of predominately black students from five area high schools every ten weeks. Time is allotted each week for the development of oral communication skills, and the most consistently successful technique has been the oral interpretation of poetry.

White teachers in predominately black groups must be knowledgeable about minority literature, and those teachers with skimpy backgrounds in minority writing should spend time in private study or in a university course to familiarize themselves with the recurring themes of freedom of expression and development of a positive self-concept. These themes have a special meaning for students of all races who have been frustrated in school because they have not met expected criteria. In addition, the study of minority literature broadens our awareness of the full gamut of contributions to the American literary heritage. As Robert Hayden, David Burrows, and Frederick Lapides state, "Afro-American literature encompasses aspects of the human condition in general and of the Negro condition in particular not otherwise articulated in American writing."[1]

Initially we tried reading excerpts from short stories in class, but it was the language of poetry that stimulated the imagination and, in turn, interest. The oral interpretation of black and other minority poetry produced the following results. Students had the opportunity to practice speaking standard English in contrast to their community dialect. They tended to gain confidence through oral reading, and the techniques of oral interpretation tended to improve all of their oral reading. Like all students of literature, they developed an understanding of the poet's purpose, an appreciation of the language, and knowledge about authors and their historical times. Finally, the themes in the poetry they read provided alternatives for identification as they searched for their own values.

Success in oral interpretation of poetry is best achieved by building on one positive experience after another. We structured the poetry unit so that the whole class initially worked with several poems; individual selections of poems came later. A short and rhythmic poem like "We Real Cool" by Gwendolyn Brooks is a good poem to start with. After a practice reading by the group, a leader is chosen to snap fingers for a beat, and the group rereads the poem to this beat. Next, the class is divided into sections and assigned particular lines, with the whole class joining in on the word "We." The mood may be changed abruptly by stopping the clicking before the pensive "Die soon." If there is room, the class or small group might do a rhythmic walk to the poem, maintaining the finger clicks. Time should be allotted for discussing the different voices in the poem.

Once the poem has captured student interest, the mechanics of oral interpretation can be introduced. Changes in meaning can be demonstrated by varying force, rate, emphasis, inflection, or pitch of the voice or by using pauses. Sentences like "Let's go to the game tonight" or "I will always remember the look on the teacher's face" can be read in numerous ways. Books on oral interpretation suggest many additional exercises.[2]

A second poem that has proved successful with basic skills students is "Dream Variation" by Langston Hughes. This poem will dictate a change in the rate and force of voice. The group may serve as a chorus for appropriate inflections, pauses, and word coloring. Lines like "Fling my arms wide" and "Dance! Whirl! Whirl!" will suggest movement. A tape recording can be made of a choral reading and played back to the students. Their performance should improve in subsequent recordings, and the repetition is of special help to students with poor reading skills.

The class is now ready for a more difficult poem like "We Wear the Mask" by Paul Laurence Dunbar, an appropriate poem for dealing with self-concept. The post-Civil War resentment among blacks who had just obtained freedom from slavery should be discussed, including the reasons for this resentment. In the reading of the poem, voice quality can be changed to express the contrast between servitude and sarcasm. Further discussion of the masks people wear leads to a session on value clarification and support activities.

Universality of theme is exemplified in Claude McKay's "If We Must Die," a poem that was quoted by Winston Churchill during a speech to the U.S. Congress after World War II. Difficult vocabulary terms should be defined and pronounced in advance, but students will gain confidence in using the words through repetition.

Robert Hayden's "Runagate Runagate" provides opportunities for solo readers: individual slaves, a plantation owner, Harriet Tubman, and so forth. Various divisions of the class may be tried, and all students might chant "Runagate Runagate," imitating the sound of train wheels on tracks. The analogy with the Underground Railroad should be explored.

The poet's background and the purpose and historical setting of each poem should be discussed in class. A time line on which each poem is placed is an easy way for students to see relationships. For example, students may perceive the contrasts among early religious themes of the eighteenth century, the themes of the Harlem Renaissance period, and the more modern "black is beautiful" theme.

Now students are ready to choose individual poems for interpretation. Each student should analyze the poem he or she has chosen by finding biographical information about the poet, by placing the poem on a historical time line, by deciding on the poet's purpose, and by defining difficult vocabulary found in the poem. Many poetry books and copies of individual poems should be available for students to use in selecting their poems.

Following a review in class of the mechanics of oral interpretation, students should be encouraged to coach each other. If feasible, they should practice with tape recorders. After sufficient preparation time, each student presents a poem to the class—introducing the poem and the poet, establishing the mood, and reading the poem. The class should make encouraging comments about the presentation. Subsequently, the teacher should provide the student with a written critique.

During one ten-week session of the CETA project, students had such a positive response to the unit that a performance was planned. Parents and friends were invited for an evening of choral readings that featured individual oral interpretations and short talks about the poets. An alternative program might have students share their oral interpretations with another class.

Although the success of this activity cannot be measured as accurately as growth in reading, grammar, and arithmetic skills, improvement in oral reading and the self-confidence of students can be observed and recorded. Poetry may be an old key, but it still opens new doors for basic skills students.

Notes

1. Robert Hayden, David J. Burrows, and Frederick R. Lapides, *Afro-American Literature: An Introduction* (New York: Harcourt Brace Jovanovich, 1971), p. 2.

2. Many books on oral interpretation are available. Five particularly good books are Violet Asmuth, *Oral Interpretation and You* (Tampa, Fla.: Florida Forensic Program, 1978); Wallace A. Bacon, *The Art of Interpretation,* 3rd ed. (New York: Holt, Rinehart and Winston, 1979); Farrell Black, Ray Heidt, Barbara Hales, and Art Smith, *Creative Strategies in Oral Literature* (Dubuque, Iowa: Kendall-Hunt Publishing Co., 1975); Donald H. Ecroyd and Hilda Stahl Wagner, *Communicate Through Oral Reading* (New York: McGraw-Hill Co., 1979); and Charlotte Lee, *Speaking Of . . . Interpretation* (Glenview, Ill.: Scott, Foresman and Co., 1977).

Three for the Price of One: Poem, Story, Film

William V. Rakauskas
University of Scranton

Several years ago when I taught my first undergraduate class in Special Methods of Teaching English, I used a text written by Abraham Bernstein, *Teaching English in the High School*. In chapter 7 of that text, "The Teaching of Poetry," Bernstein described an approach he labeled "two for the price of one":

> The first suggestion in reducing the difficulty of poetry is to find a well-matched, relevant mate to the poem you plan to teach, another poem of a similar theme that will keep your poem company. You will find it easier to teach "Ozymandias" if you simultaneously teach it with Holmes' "The Deacon's Masterpiece" or MacLeish's "You, Andrew Marvell" because all three have a common theme, the passing evanescence of mortal things; "Miniver Cheevy" with "Richard Cory" because of the common theme of flight and escape . . . ; Tennyson's "Crossing the Bar" (with its peaceful acquiescence to death) and Dylan Thomas' "Do Not Go Gentle into That Good Night" (quite the opposite!)[1]

I liked the approach and used it in my course in basic composition. Pleased with the satisfying reception given the method by my students, I encouraged my student teachers to develop "two-for-the-price-of-one" strategies of their own. This they did, and in my observations of their practice teaching in the local high school classrooms I saw clever variations created by these future teachers. These students paired not only poem with poem but also short story with short story, novel with novel, and essay with essay. Their ideas inspired me to begin some serious experimenting and adapting of my own. In so doing I eventually developed what I call my "three for the price of one" technique.

Selecting a poem, short story, and film with parallel themes, I work with my students on techniques of analysis of different literary types, on writing about various forms of literature, and on cross-genre comparisons.

One of my "three-for-the-price-of-one" sets outlined in this article includes the poem "Pigeon Woman," by May Swenson, the short story

173

"Miss Brill," by Katherine Mansfield, and the short, seventeen-minute film "The String Bean."

"Pigeon Woman" is a forty-line narrative poem about a woman who feeds pigeons at exactly 1:30 each day in front of the public library. After first questioning the title, we read the poem together as a class, attempting to identify facts about the woman. Then, we try to separate facts from what we infer from the poem's images. We determine, for example, that without fail the woman arrives at the same scene each day at 1:30:

> Slate, or dirty-marble-colored,
> or rusty-iron-colored, the pigeons
> on the flagstones in front of the
> Public Library make a sharp lake
> into which the pigeon woman wades
> at exactly 1:30.

We also know much about the way she dresses:

> . . . She wears a
> plastic pink raincoat with a round
> collar (looking like a little
> girl, so gay) and flat gym shoes,
> her hair square-cut, orange.

The poet establishes the imagery early in the poem, ". . . the pigeons . . . make a sharp lake." Through a series of questions, through constant reference to the details of the poem, and through ongoing discussions, we observe how the poet continues the image of the pigeon lake in stanza two (the pigeon woman *"wades"*), in stanza three ("the spinning, crooning *waves*") in stanza six ("choppy, shadowy *ripples*"), and in stanza eight (*"drain* away in an untouchable *tide"*).

At both the beginning and at the end of the poem, the lake image suggests something cutting ("sharp lake/flints of love"). Throughout the rest of the poem, the image is soothing and comfortable ("crooning waves/shadowy ripples"). Then, in stanza eight, the image becomes a rejecting one: the waters "drain away in an untouchable tide."

As students pay close attention to the diction of the poem, they come to realize what the poet is trying to do. They inductively conclude that word choice is significant in image creation and that the function of imagery is to evoke in them responses out of their own experience. Even though the experience in the fictional world of the poem may be foreign to them, they can, nevertheless, easily imagine how such an experience would make them feel. Therefore, they are able to re-create vicariously the rejection experienced by the lonely old pigeon woman.

What we are doing, of course, is becoming aware of the fact that the poem's effect depends upon the poet's careful use of conventional devices, upon the precise detailing of important scenes, and, most especially, upon the choice of words used to establish images and to provide data from which meaningful inferences can be drawn.

Making inferences, drawing conclusions from available evidence, is an important part of the classroom activity. I explain to the students that our "educated guesses" might occasionally be inaccurate, but if we pay attention to what the poem offers, we can come to a reasonable interpretation of the poem's theme. Here for example, from the facts emphasized and the images presented, we infer that the woman is lonely, that she buys a few moments of love from the pigeons by giving them bread, and that she is disappointed because she is not loved after she has nothing to offer. We can be reasonably certain, also, that despite her being rejected, she will return to the pigeon lake before the public library again and again, for she needs to feel some kind of animate love.

Next the class and I turn to Katherine Mansfield's short story "Miss Brill." Although we are now working with a different literary type, some of the same considerations given the poem will be under focus and discussion as we work with this story. As with our study of the poem, here too we must pay attention to detail, to fact, to images:

> Miss Brill was glad that she had decided on her fur. The air was motionless, but when you opened your mouth there was a faint chill . . . . She had taken it out of its box that afternoon . . . .

At the park the season had begun, and although the band played all year round, it was never the same. "It was like someone playing with only the family to listen to." Two people shared her special seat this Sunday but did not speak, and their not speaking disappointed Miss Brill for she looked forward to eavesdropping; in fact, she "had become really quite expert . . . at listening . . . at sitting in other people's lives."

What are the facts here? Miss Brill is an odd person; she is not communicative; she does not lead an exciting life of her own. Often, she fantasizes, imagining herself to be part of the park scene:

> O, how fascinating it was . . . . How she loved sitting here, watching it all! It was like a play, it was exactly like a play . . . . Even she had a part and came every Sunday. No doubt somebody would have noticed if she hadn't been there; she was part of the performance. . . . She was on stage.

Miss Brill has nothing; she is a lonely human being imagining herself part of the scene at the Jardins Publiques. She is a nobody. She has no one, and no one really cares about her. Any joy she receives from life is supplied by her imagination and by her pride in her worn, dim fur.

A return to the opening paragraph of the story gives us a chance to reread the description of Miss Brill's handling of her precious fur:

> She had taken it out of its box that afternoon, shaken out the moth powder, given it a good brush, and rubbed the life back into the dim little eyes . . . . But the nose, which was of some black composition, wasn't at all firm. It must have had a knock, somehow. Never mind—a little dab of black sealing wax when the time came—when it was absolutely necessary.

Just as the image of the pigeon lake provided the emotional tenor in Swenson's "Pigeon Woman," here the fur serves as the vehicle to carry the tenor of Mansfield's "Miss Brill." The shabby fur is, for Miss Brill, something special. It is Miss Brill's fertile imagination that makes the fur beautiful, just as it is her imagination that makes her life tolerable. Her fur is the one possession that truly brings her occasional joy. But her happiness in the park with her fur is marginal and fleeting. Her eavesdropping makes her vulnerable, and when she hears the insensitive young lovers refer to her as the "stupid old thing at the end there," she is simply hurt, but when Miss Brill hears the giggling girl say, "It's her fu-fur which is so funny. . . . It's exactly like a fried whiting," she is devastated.

She rushes home, sits down on her red eiderdown, unclasps the necklet of the fur, and quickly, without looking, lays the fur inside of the box from which she had so lovingly taken it earlier that day. Placing the lid on the box, she thinks she hears something crying.

The woman has been hurt. The one thing that had brought her fleeting joy has now been packed away. The story ends abruptly at this point, and we are left to imagine the life that the lonely and vulnerable Miss Brill will have in future seasons.

It is time now for making comparisons and for gleaning some ideas for writing about the poem and the story. Several topics for essays are apparent. For example, "In what ways are the pigeon woman and Miss Brill alike/different?" (Both are vulnerable. Both get hurt. However, the tenacious pigeon woman continues to return each day to feed the motley pigeons, the pigeons for whom "she colors her own feathers." Even though she is disappointed when she is not loved after she has nothing to offer, she returns each day to buy a few moments of love from the pigeons by giving them bread. Her life remains tolerable. Not so with Miss Brill. There will be no more joys after the insults she has experienced. She will probably not return again to the Jardins Publiques wearing her seasonal fur. Her life becomes intolerable.)

Some other topics for writing include the following: "Discuss the imagery in each work." Respond to the questions, "Who is the stronger woman?" "What additional inferences can be drawn from the poem?" "From the story?" "With whom do you sympathize more?" "Do you know any person like the pigeon woman or Miss Brill?"

Like the thirteenth doughnut in a baker's dozen, the short film "The String Bean" completes the triad. This seventeen-minute film, which I borrow from our public library, is the simple story of a frail old woman living alone in an austere apartment. Because no dialogue accompanies the film, the viewer must make from what the film shows many inferences about the woman's past, her present condition, and her probable future. Very significant is the fact that the film switches from black and white to color during critical moments in a woman's day. Visual foreshadowing and color symbolism are two technical elements for student attention during the film, for class discussion after the film, and for essay topics during compositional follow-up activities.

A brief review of the film will indicate the areas of similarity and difference among the different genres under consideration. The wispy old woman in the film leaves her dreary apartment one day for a walk to the park. On her way back she takes from a rubbish can a string bean plant. When she gets home, she removes the bean seeds from the plant and prepares them for planting in a flowerpot.

As the film progresses, she cultivates a potted string bean with tender and loving care. Her only diversion from her monotonous life in her tidy, dingy apartment is to water and to sun her green plant. When it finally sprouts, she carries it each day to the sunny park, places the plant near her bench and carefully watches over it as a mother might watch over a child. Each day she returns with the plant to her room and puts it away for the night.

One day, when the plant has outgrown the pot, the old woman takes her daily visit to the park and plants the common string bean plant in a beautiful flowerbed in the park. A park gardener discovers the plant, thinks it is nothing but an unwanted weed that has no place among the beautiful park flowers, rips it out of its bed, and tosses it away. This is not the first time that the persistent woman has had to come to the plant's rescue, but this time it is too late, for the plant has been uprooted. Undaunted, however, the woman plucks the beans from the torn-up plant, returns home, and plants the new beans in her flowerpot. Outside the rain falls, the woman smiles, and we know she will soon have a new green friend.

What are the similarities among the three pieces—the poem, the short story, the film? Each involves a lonely old woman—one who returns each day to the public library to feed the pigeons, one who visits the Jardins Publiques each Sunday in a fur that is precious to her, and one who visits a park daily with her string bean plant. Each is hurt in some way—the pigeons reject the pigeon woman after her daily offering is made; the young insensitive couple shatters Miss Brill's fantasy world with their comments about her fur, and the string bean woman has a plant that means so much to her ripped from the nourishing ground in which she had transferred it.

Differences? The most essential difference among the three occurs at the conclusion of each work and concerns the attitude and probable future of each woman. Despite rejection, the pigeon woman will still visit the park at 1:30 each day; there is nothing else to replace the need she has for animate contact. Miss Brill will probably not return again on Sundays in season to her special bench in the Jardins; her world has been shattered beyond repair. And the string bean woman, the most optimistic one of all, will continue to nourish her simple green plant.

As Ouida Clapp points out in *Classroom Practices in Teaching English, 1977–1978: Teaching the Basics—Really!* "Experience has shown that the greater the activity with language, the better and more lasting results. . . . Along with listening, speaking, reading, writing, and appreciating literature, they [students] must be taught in contexts that guarantee a continuous reinforcement of each skill by the others."[2] And this is precisely what is happening here. The total involvement of the students in the explication process, in the discussion periods, and in writing activities enables them to learn basic analytical skills, to appreciate fully the artistry of the poet, the short story author, and the film maker as each communicates a thesis. Finally, the "three-for-the-price-of-one" approach affords them opportunities to synthesize in writing the results of their analysis and discussion.

Notes

1. Abraham Bernstein, *Teaching English in High School* (New York: Random House, 1968), p. 232.

2. Ouida Clapp, chair, and the NCTE Committee on Classroom Practices in Teaching English, *Classroom Practices in Teaching English, 1977–1978: Teaching the Basics—Really!* (Urbana, Ill.: NCTE, 1977), p. xii.

References

Mansfield, Katherine. "Miss Brill," in *Literature: Structure, Sound, and Sense,* ed. Laurence Perrine. New York: Harcourt Brace Jovanovich, 1972), pp. 450–53.

Roberts, Edgar V. *Writing Themes about Literature.* Englewood Cliffs, N.J.: Prentice-Hall, 1977.

Swenson, May. "Pigeon Woman," in Fred Morgan, *Here and Now II: An Approach to Writing through Perception.* New York: Harcourt Brace Jovanovich, 1972, pp. 88–89.